DAN THE AUTOMATOR PRESENTS 2K7

CD IN STORES SEPTEMBER 19TH

EXCLUSIVE NEW MUSIC PRODUCED BY **DAN THE AUTOMATOR** FEATURING:

FABOLOUS ★ GHOSTFACE ★ SLIM THUG ★ E-40 ★ LUPE FIASCO
MOS DEF ★ A TRIBE CALLED QUEST ★ RHYMEFEST
HIEROGLYPHICS ★ EVIDENCE & RAAKA OF DILATED PEOPLES
CHARLI 2NA OF JURASSIC 5 ★ ACEYALONE ★ ZION I
A.G. OF D.I.T.C. ★ ANWAR SUPERSTAR

DECON

ALSO ON DECON DECONMEDIA.COM

ACEYALONE & RJD2
MAGNIFICENT CITY

RJD2
MAGNIFICENT CITY INSTRUMENTS

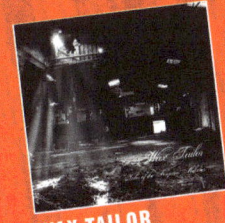
WAX TAILOR
TALES OF THE FORGOTTEN MELODIES

A-TEAM
WHO REFRAMED THE A-TEAM

FINE-TUNED INSTRUMENT.

FINE-TUNED INSTRUMENT_ 2.0

With the Continuously Variable Transmission (CVT), we eliminated shift shock for a cool performance. With available Bluetooth® hands-free capability and the Intelligent Key, we arranged high-tech melodies into harmonious convenience. The next generation of Nissan thinking in the next Nissan Maxima. **NissanUSA.com**

The Next Nissan Maxima

SHIFT_ 2.0

Nissan, the Nissan Brand Symbol, "SHIFT_" tagline and Nissan model names are Nissan trademarks. Always wear your seat belt, and please don't drink and drive. ©2006 Nissan North America, Inc.

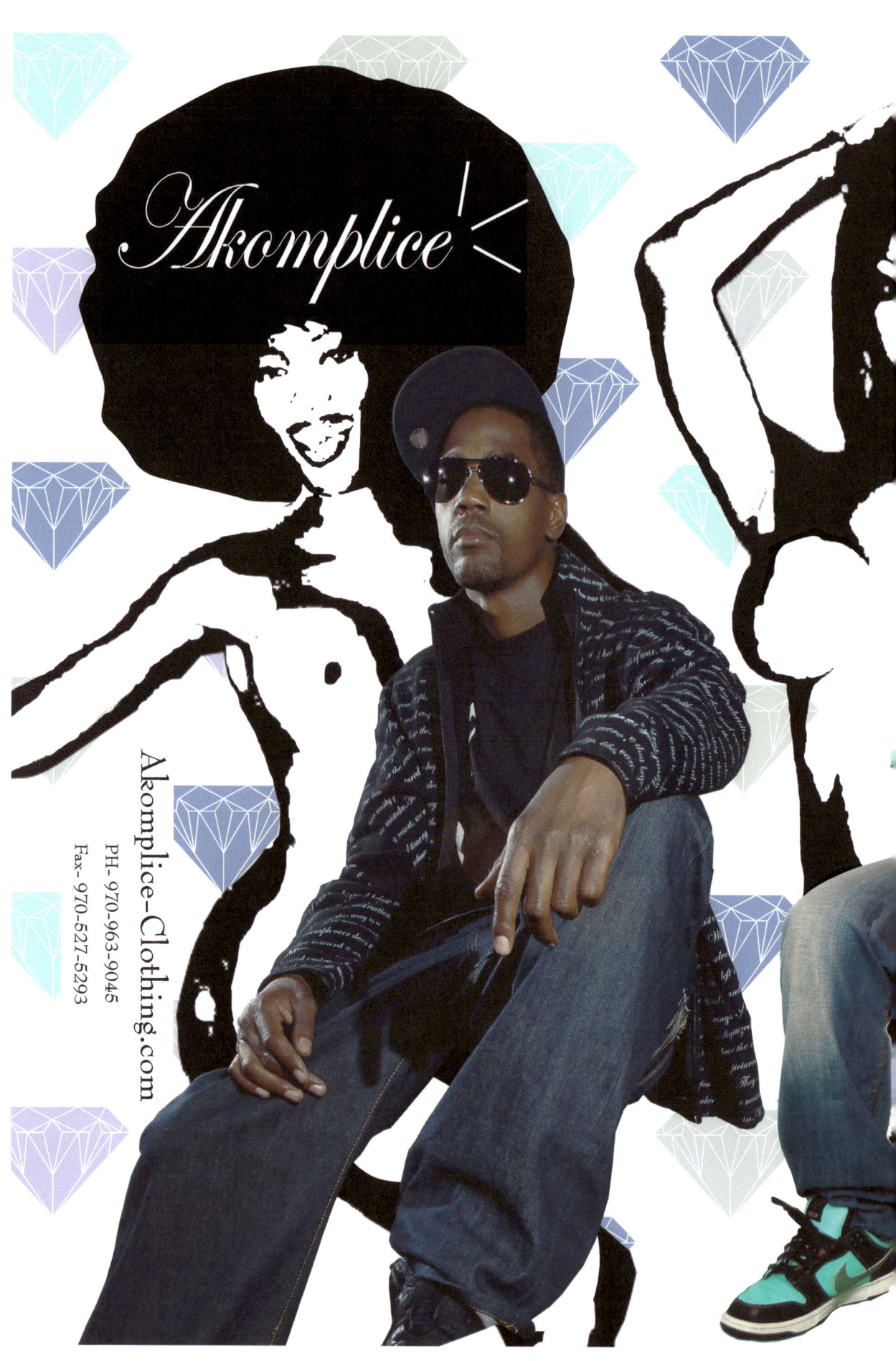

Table of Contents

Wax Poetics, Issue #18, Aug/Sept 2006

Re:Discovery: the new classics	012
Rapper Yo Gotti got Memphis soul	022
Memphis rappers on the hustle	024
Obituary: Ronald Clyne, Folkways Records designer	026
Brazilian superstar Ed Motta's vinyl jones	030
The P-Funk Saga Begins	036
The Parliaments	042
Billy "Bass" Nelson and the rise of Funkadelic	058
Mr. Bernie (Worrell) goes to Parliament (Funkadelic)	070
The beautiful mind of Funkadelic artist Pedro Bell	082
From Cincinnati to the P-Funk omniverse	090
Frankie "Kash" Waddy and his Mothership connections	094
The name is Bootsy, baby	100
Garry Shider and his bop gun	112
Artist Overton Lloyd captures a motor booty affair	118
George Clinton's cosmic journey	124
Audio Heritage: recorded media	136

Photo by Richard Edson.

waxpoetics

Published by	Wax Poetics
Editor-in-Chief	Andre Torres
Editor	Brian DiGenti
Creative Director	Kevin DeBernardi
Marketing Director	Dennis Coxen
Contributing Editors	Dante Carfagna John Paul Jones Andrew Mason
Contributing Photo Editor	B+
Sales and Marketing Manager	Michael Coxen
Accounts Manager	Joy DiGenti
Copy Editor	Tom McClure
Interns	P. J. Azzara, Alex Biedermann, Gabe Millman, Ed Ntiri, Julien-Pierre Schmitz, Wallace Simpson, James Steiner, Dominic Wagner
Contributing Writers	Brandon Burke, Robbie Busch, Dante Carfagna, Richard Edson, Thomas Sayers Ellis, Edward Hill, Sam Hopkins, Gareth Jones, Andria Lisle, Matt Rogers, James Steiner, Raymond Tyler, Oliver Wang
Contributing Photographers	Jackson Bezerra, Justin Burks, Richard Edson, Patrick Gherdoussi, Matt Rogers
Contributing Artists	Jean-Yves Blanc, Alberto Forero

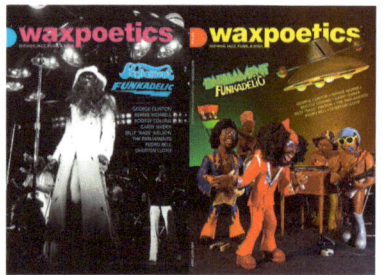

Cover: Models by Jean-Yves Blanc (hiphopsculpture.com) for Wax Poetics, 2006. Photo by Patrick Gherdoussi.

Back: George Clinton and Parliament's Mothership Tour, 1977. Photo © Michael Ochs Archives.com

Errata: In Issue 17's "12 x 12," we reported that Michael "Sugar Bear" Foreman was the bassist/bandleader for E.U. and played on John Davis and the Monster Orchestra's "I Can't Stop." However, Greg "Sugar Bear" Elliot was the bassist/bandleader for E.U., while Michael "Sugar Bear" Foreman was the bassist for MFSB (and played on "I Can't Stop"). We regret the error. Thanks for checkin' us.

ISBN 978-0-9992127-9-0
© 2006, 2020 Wax Poetics

Originally published Aug/Sept 2006

Published by Wax Poetics Books
Printed by Lightning Source

All rights reserved.
Unauthorized duplication without prior written consent is prohibited.

The first time I heard Parliament-Funkadelic play, I wasn't shocked by the infusion of rock into the music. It seemed like a natural progression to me, because what they were doing, the Rolling Stones were trying to do. What they were doing, Eric Clapton and people were trying to do. Although, Eric and those people were trying to do it from more of a blues base, and Parliament-Funkadelic didn't have to do that; they came from that. So they were naturally taking it somewhere else further. Theirs was really a bringing together of rock and funk, and the feel was exactly right.
—Nona Hendryx in *One Nation Under a Groove*, 2005 PBS documentary on P-Funk

Nona ain't lying either, the feel was exactly right—still is really. Who would have thought that a few brothas doing hair in a New Jersey barbershop could start waving their freak flags high and change the course of music history? But that's exactly what George Clinton and his U.S. Funk Mob did. But do a search for the greatest rock bands of all time, and you won't see mention of Parliament-Funkadelic. Now, I know that rock critics like to fight over whether the Rolling Stones or the Beatles deserve the number-one spot, but, in my eyes, neither of them can hold a candle to what P-Funk brought to the music.

I'm not fronting on the Beatles, the Rolling Stones, or Led Zeppelin; they were cool. But, as far as I'm concerned, P-Funk rocked harder than all of them combined. And they were funkier than all three combined, which puts it over the edge for me. But George and crew's music oozes with soul; you can feel the funk in everything they do, from the dirty fuzz of Funkadelic, to the fresh and clean crispness of Parliament. These brothas couldn't just rock shit, they could also smooth it out and make it bump. Even in their finest boogie hour, the Stones' "Miss You" can't stand next to "Flash Light." So while most critics want to put the holy trinity on a pedestal, with the world domination of hip-hop culture and the large role that P-Funk has played in the sound of hip-hop music, I dare say that P-Funk's impact can be felt much more strongly thirty years later than any of those three bands. When I asked Dr. Dre, the quintessential post-modern producer who has changed the course of pop music three times in two decades, who he listened to growing up and was his biggest influence, he said Parliament-Funkadelic. Not the Beatles.

But it's funny that the greatest rock group is always assumed to be White (though many of the greatest things are assumed to be White, but that's another book altogether). I had to check with a white friend to make sure I wasn't going to come off sounding funny. But my man had something interesting to say: "The idea that you could be racist talking about a genre that stole all its elements and wildly profited from Black music is ludicrous." Right on. Then he dropped the bomb: "Jimmy Page suing Schoolly D is racist!" Right on two times, my brother. Think about it: Led Zeppelin and Page make a career of "borrowing" from Black music, then when a Black artist like Schoolly D samples "Kashmir" for "Signifying Rapper" and uses it in Abel Ferrara's brilliant *Bad Lieutenant*, he wants to sue. Dude's got some nerve; he should be the last one accusing someone of stealing. He had to hit a number of people off that he stole from over the years, including Howlin' Wolf and Willie Dixon. I should point out that Page did agree to replay the riff for Diddy's wack-ass track on the *Godzilla* soundtrack though. I guess money talks.

So these cats can keep assembling their lists; I got my own. At the top is Parliament-Funkadelic, the greatest rock and roll band of all time. Like the P-Funk Mob, we know about being the freaks of the industry. Every year, they assemble more lists about the best music magazines and we haven't topped one yet, but there isn't a music magazine out there giving it up like Wax Poetics, so we know who's at the top of our list. It's cool; we don't need them telling us what's up anyway. While they're all busy patting each other on the back talking about the greatest rock group or the best magazine, we'll be here writing our story.

Fly on sistas, play on brothas,

Andre Torres
Editor-in-Chief

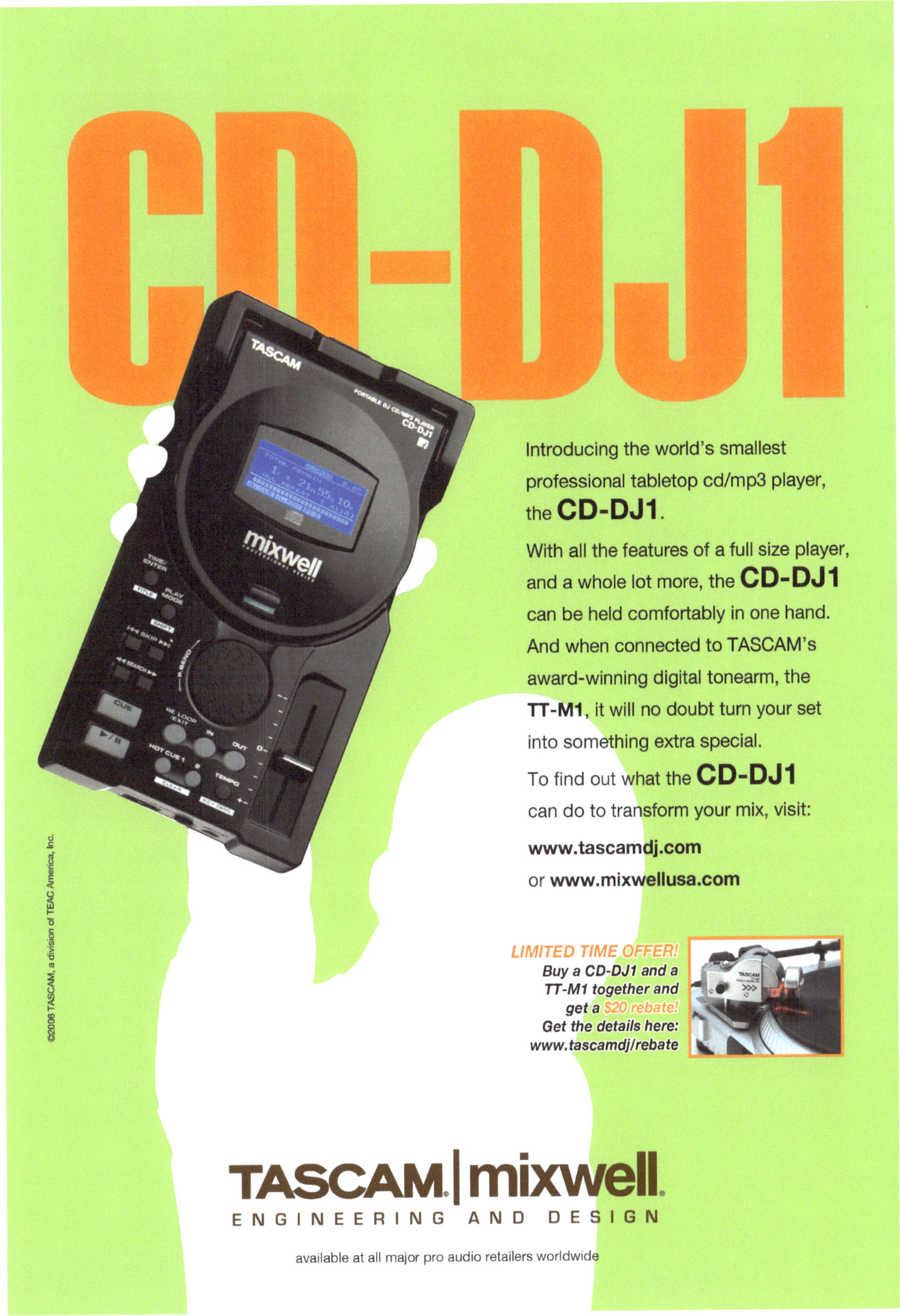

CD-DJ1

Introducing the world's smallest professional tabletop cd/mp3 player, the **CD-DJ1**.

With all the features of a full size player, and a whole lot more, the **CD-DJ1** can be held comfortably in one hand. And when connected to TASCAM's award-winning digital tonearm, the **TT-M1**, it will no doubt turn your set into something extra special.

To find out what the **CD-DJ1** can do to transform your mix, visit:

www.tascamdj.com
or **www.mixwellusa.com**

LIMITED TIME OFFER!
Buy a CD-DJ1 and a TT-M1 together and get a $20 rebate!
Get the details here:
www.tascamdj/rebate

TASCAM | mixwell
ENGINEERING AND DESIGN

available at all major pro audio retailers worldwide

reDISCOVERY

Too many men on the goddamn field. This pep record would have been a victor's memento if not for a miscue on a two-point conversion in the 1969 Orange Bowl. Nevertheless, soul singers the Tips, of Lawrence, Kansas, teamed up in the run-up to the big game with Gary Jackson and the Soul Messengers. The result was the best—and only—fan funk I've ever come across, and they're singing about my alma mater.

The University of Kansas (KU) Jayhawks have always been best known for basketball prowess. But, for a quick spell in the Age of Aquarius, the Hawks achieved some gridiron glory, and the Tips cheered them on with a Pigmeat-esque "Year he [sic], the game's in session. Now here come the Hawks." A bass breakdown chases the intro, taking us to the "Here come the Hawks, y'all" chorus. The drums aren't loud enough, but the vocals compensate in the foreground with a bleacher-based exuberance that answers the setup question "Hey, man, who's the Hawks?" with, of course, "They're #1." No date on the record, but being "Miami-bound" and "going where the oranges grow" laid me a Sherlock trail. And since the Orange Bowl was played on January 1, 1969, the record must date from late 1968.

Artist: The Tips backed by Gary Jackson and the Soul Messengers
Record: "Hawk It to 'Em" (b/w "If I Say...")
Label: Audio House (AHP 15568)
Release: 1968

While I was still at KU in recent years, an abominable pop-rap version of the school's "Rock Chalk" chant circulated ahead of the NCAA hoops tournament. It was no doubt recorded in someone's apartment, and the talent displayed is nowhere close to this '68 effort. The Tips & Co. cut this groove at Lawrence's Audio House studio, responsible for a few other notable Larryville sides. As for the artists, they could have ended up in Vietnam or just headed out of town after graduating.

It's rumored that only fifty copies were pressed, all on blue vinyl with a crimson label, owing to KU's colors. It has sold on eBay as a "northern-soul rarity" for a hefty bid. But to me, "Hawk It to 'Em" is priceless—the world's funkiest foam finger. If only we had won. —*Sam Hopkins*

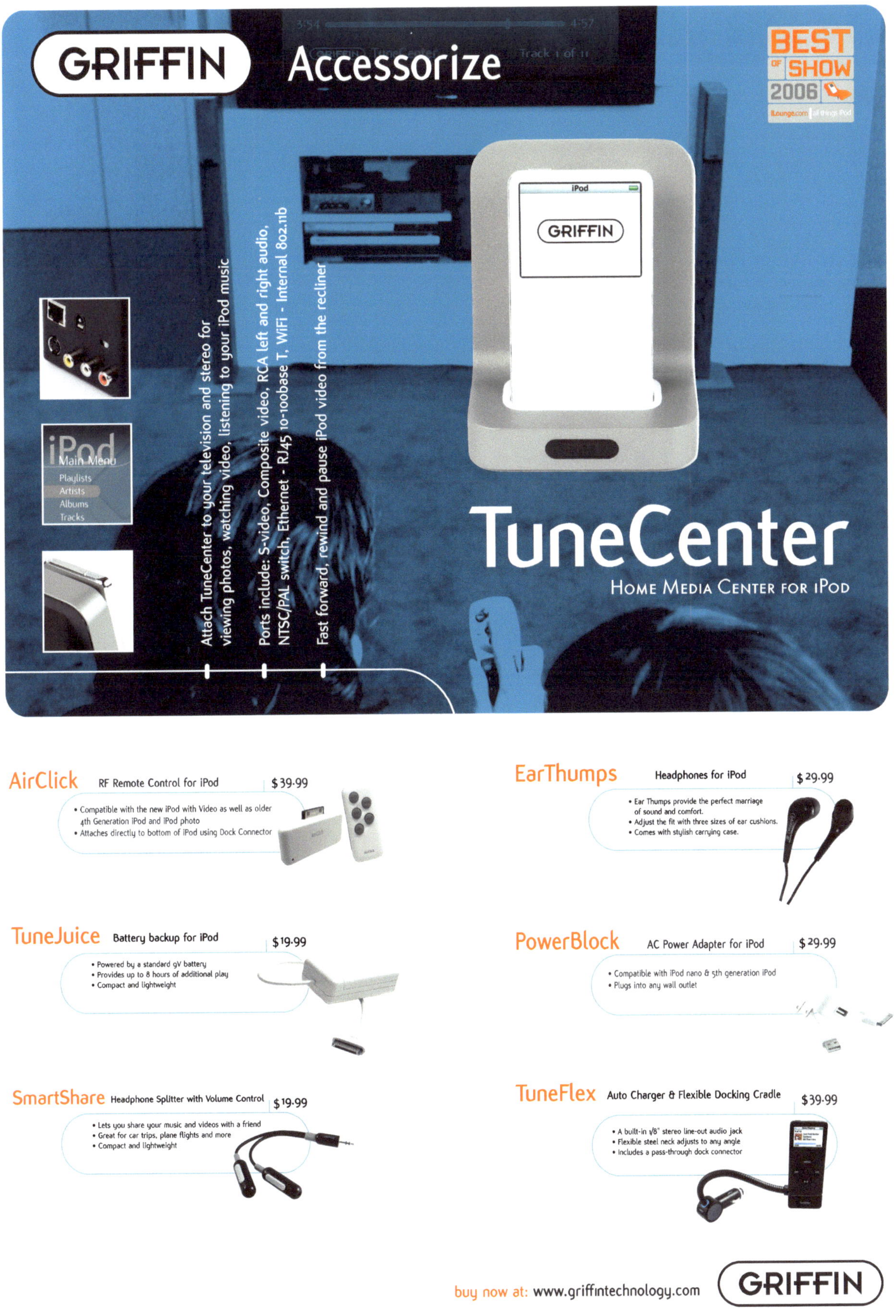

GRIFFIN Accessorize

BEST OF SHOW 2006
iLounge.com all things iPod

TuneCenter
HOME MEDIA CENTER FOR iPod

Attach TuneCenter to your television and stereo for viewing photos, watching video, listening to your iPod music

Ports include: S-video, Composite video, RCA left and right audio, NTSC/PAL switch, RJ45 10-100base T, WiFi - Internal 802.11b

Fast forward, rewind and pause iPod video from the recliner

AirClick — RF Remote Control for iPod — $39.99
- Compatible with the new iPod with Video as well as older 4th Generation iPod and iPod photo
- Attaches directly to bottom of iPod using Dock Connector

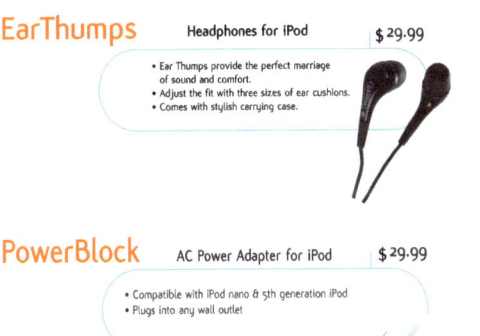

EarThumps — Headphones for iPod — $29.99
- Ear Thumps provide the perfect marriage of sound and comfort.
- Adjust the fit with three sizes of ear cushions.
- Comes with stylish carrying case.

TuneJuice — Battery backup for iPod — $19.99
- Powered by a standard 9V battery
- Provides up to 8 hours of additional play
- Compact and lightweight

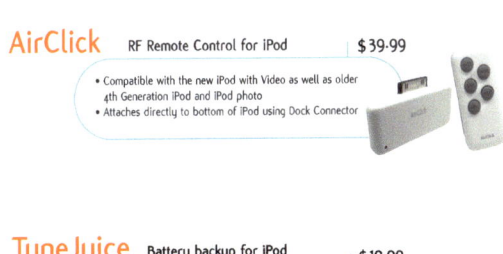

PowerBlock — AC Power Adapter for iPod — $29.99
- Compatible with iPod nano & 5th generation iPod
- Plugs into any wall outlet!

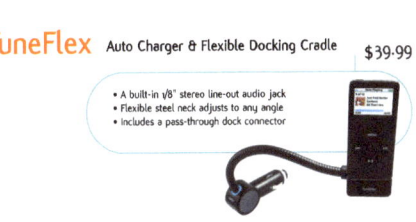

SmartShare — Headphone Splitter with Volume Control — $19.99
- Lets you share your music and videos with a friend
- Great for car trips, plane flights and more
- Compact and lightweight

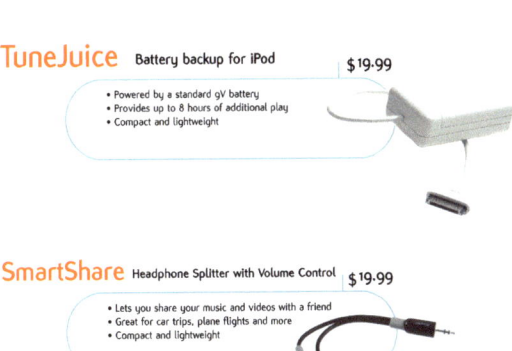

TuneFlex — Auto Charger & Flexible Docking Cradle — $39.99
- A built-in 1/8" stereo line-out audio jack
- Flexible steel neck adjusts to any angle
- Includes a pass-through dock connector

buy now at: www.griffintechnology.com

GRIFFIN

"Puddin'" is far from the deepest or most brilliant disco single ever conceived, but it ranks amongst the more quirky. For one, it's unusual to see too many disco singles armed with a picture cover—let alone on a private imprint—and you have to enjoy the uber-'70s decor and fashion that Belle Farms Estate (both the name of the group and label) are rocking here. The cover sticker crows, "Baltimore's own 'cause Baltimore's best," and the assembled band is presumably all local (drummer Larry Jeter now runs the city's Dimensions in Music record store). Of the gathered players, only writer, arranger, and producer Maynard Parker saw much national acclaim—he made a small name for himself in the early 1970s as a session guitarist for Prestige Records, playing on several of Charles Earland's albums and overseeing his 1973 solo LP, *Midnight Rider*.

Together, the Estate knock out an entertainingly funky tune whose slightly lo-fi quality is balanced by its bright, upbeat appeal. The rhythm section—led by Wesley James's percussive elements, Eric Perry's steady bass lines, and the smooth, soft touches of Dave Barnes's electric piano—locks the groove down, while Parker's guitar work riffs just under the surface, content to play with the rhythm rather than over it. What's notable is that the single offers up not one, not two, but three different versions of the song, each one steadily longer. The shortest, at 3.5 minutes, is over too quickly, but the 5.5 minute version not only gives you more time to get your puddin' on but adds in loud hand claps that help anchor the disco beat. The monster is the B-side—nearly eleven minutes long—which includes a long keyboard solo by Barnes missing from the shorter siblings.

Artist: Belle Farms Estate
Record: "Puddin'"
Label: Belle Farms Estate
Release: 1976

Mostly, though, we just love the title and main chorus: "Puddin's my true love/ puddin's my whole life." It's not at all clear what vocalist Ethel Meyers is singing about—we'd guess it was something sexual, but, somehow, the song just doesn't give off that vibe. But, hey, we're down with the idea of puddin' being our whole life *and* true love even if we have no idea what that means. –Oliver Wang

BMS001

JEAN-CLAUDE VANNIER
L'ENFANT ASSASSIN DES MOUCHES

FROM THE ARRANGER OF "L'HISTOIRE DE MELODY NELSON" COMES THE PSYCHEDELIC SYMPHONY THAT INSPIRED THE WRITINGS OF SERGE GAINSBOURG (FEATURING EXCLUSIVE BONUS VINTAGE VIDEO FOOTAGE)

"The French David Axelrod" Q magazine 4/5
"J.C.V is a f*****g genius! DAVID HOLMES
"Haunted by the ghost of Gainsbourg this record is real, you really need it."
JARVIS COCKER (PULP)
"This kind of record could not be made today: who would pay for this brilliant suite of instrumental concrete madness?"
JIM O'ROURKE (SONIC YOUTH)

BOTH RELEASED ON 09/19/06

BMS002

SUSAN CHRISTIE
PAINT A LADY

INCREDIBLE VINTAGE FOLK-FUNK MONSTER TAKEN FROM UNRELEASED ACETATE!

"Brings me back to the early days of my youth, sitting around the living room with my dad, listening to dusty folk LPs while he smoked a joint or three. Except this sh*t sounds like Madlib produced it."

EGON (Now Again Records)

COMING SOON..........................
MEGA-RARE VINTAGE TURKISH
B-BOY INSTRUMENTAL LP
'MUSTAFA OZKENT - GENÇLIK ILE ELELE'

B Music is an independent collective of DJs, musicians, and music lovers dedicated to the obsessive and painstaking pursuit of obscure, obsolete, exquisitely obnoxious, unbelievable, underexposed and undeniably delectable discs of experimental pop music from the psyched out 60's and 70's and beyond.

Centered around a global eponymous traveling club and a home base residency in Manchester UK (spearheaded by Andy Votel and Dominic Thomas) with a newfound habitat in NYC:

B-Music has evolved to embrace the triple-label aesthete of the Finders Keepers, Delay 68, and Twisted Nerve labels while representing a passionate, un-blinkered approach to the culmination of way-out sounds, bugged-out cinema, design and literature; encompassing all elements of off-kilter counter-culture.

Distributed by Caroline, NYC

www.b-music.us

reDISCOVERY

Praise be upon the sons of Dayton, Ohio, for their ingenuity has always manifested itself in the most unexpected of ways. Daytonites Orville and Wilbur Wright fashioned the first aircraft in the image of a bicycle, not, as Da Vinci would have had it, in that of a bird. Walter "Junie" Morrison, synth aficionado and leader of Dayton's Ohio Players, revolutionized the funk bass line by a similarly deranged twist of logic. Junie realized that—in a funky inversion of the play of lift and weight on a jetliner's wing—a sonorous bass bump must be set against an ear-rending synth screech in order to achieve true heaviness.

Junie has spent his entire musical career demonstrating the soundness of this principle. Galvanized by the way-back-yonder funk of Clinton & Co., Junie took the Players through three albums of ramshackle squeal and bump. While the albums *Pleasure*, *Pain*, and *Ecstasy* thrived on the tension between the Players' road-hardened R&B traditionalism and Junie's penchant for no-holds-barred experimentation, his Westbound solo albums, particularly 1975's *Freeze*, offer a glimpse of Junie at an unfettered peak of eccentricity.

Artist: Junie
Record: *Freeze*
Label: Westbound
Release: 1975

By 1975, Junie had traded in his ARP Soloist (of "Funky Worm" fame) for the Mini-Moog, the ARP String Ensemble, and the Heil Talk Box. Holed up in Memphis's Ardent Studios, the overdub-happy Junie single-handedly crafted a chaotically inspired album that looked back to the one-man-band aesthetic of Shuggie and *Riot*-era Sly, while anticipating the synthetic croak of Zapp, Prince's frenetic eclecticism, and Junie's own groundbreaking work with George Clinton and P-Funk. Clinton could not have failed to appreciate the slow-motion bounce of "Super J." or the schizoid arrangement that lay beneath the sonic pandemonium of *Freeze*'s title track; for by the close of the '70s, Clinton had made Junie one of his closest collaborators. One can detect Junie's fingerprints on much of P-Funk's synth-heavy late-'70s output, sharing the funk duties with P-Funk vet Bernie Worrell.

Laden down by its own spirit of funky invention, *Freeze* is perhaps too cluttered, too overwhelmingly bizarre, to be a masterpiece. It is instead the father of masterpieces, which may be better. ○ –James Steiner

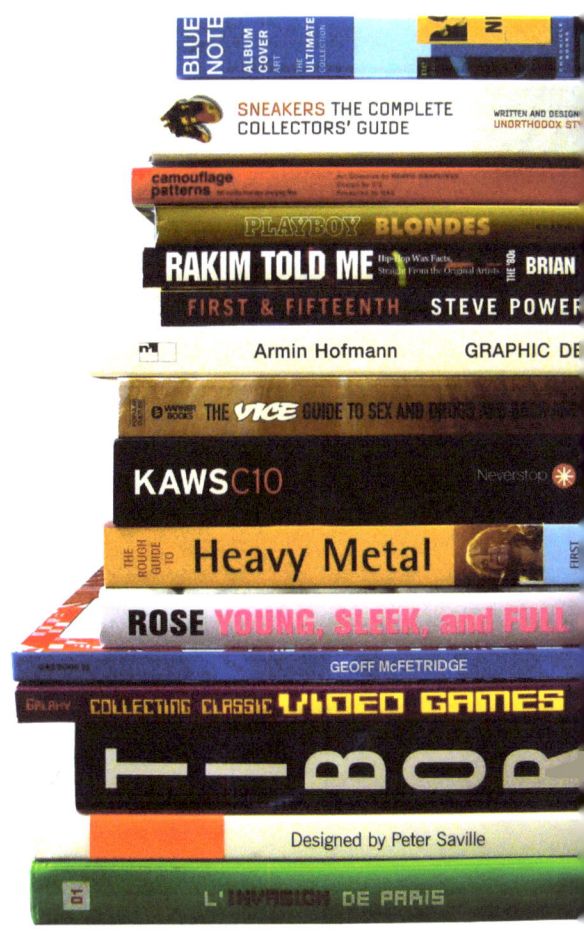

online superstore
www.turntablelab.com

turntable lab manhattan
120 east 7th st 212.677.0675

turntable lab los angeles
424 north fairfax ave 323.782.0173

TURNTABLE LAB

ReDISCOVERY

1 2 3 **4** 5

In 1989, I watched video shows and listened to the radio with blank VHS and cassette tapes ready to roll. One day, watching *The Box* before leaving for work, I saw a brother (Professor X) wearing all black with heavy African garb (ankhs and leather medallions) like the Black Israelites that piss off "the suit-and-sneaker corporate types" on the streets of New York and Philly. Professor X was smoothly but forcefully exclaiming to the camera, "We are protected by the red, the black, and the green…*sissy*!" As I listened to the opening from Parliament's classic "Flash Light" turn into a thick, muddy sample of "More Bounce to the Ounce," I hit the record button on the VCR and snatched my record list from off of my TV to add this song. I was running late to work, but the plantation be damned, I had to watch this amazing video to the end to get the name of the song and the group. On Friday, I was bugging Nino at the Funk-O-Mart (in Philadelphia) to get me "Heed the Word of the Brother" on wax.

Artist: X-Clan
Record: "Heed the Word of the Brother"
Label: 4th & Broadway
Release: 1989

When I got the record home, I put it (Garvey-side up) on my turntable. Hearing it on a better system than my ten-year-old TV, I noticed that producer Mark the 45 King had changed Roger Troutman's contemporary boogie music into a marching cadence.

Instead of marching, Brother J takes us on a three-minute-and-thirty-nine-second ride in the X-Clan's pink Caddy—sharing his perspective on being pro-Black. "I wear a crown, extension and dimension of a brain cell. Bringing hell to the sellouts," J explains. "Black is a color, while Blackness, state of a mind state." As Professor X lets us out of their ride, he adds, "Yo, Aristotle, Plato, Socrates, step off!"

Today when I scratch in Professor X's intro, "Exist in a state of Vanglorious," it still sparks something rebellious in me. For almost twenty years, "Heed the Word of the Brother" has made me think about my freedom, as well as dance. "Word to Ra." —Raymond Tyler

ReDISCOVERY

Sweet sunshine soul seeps through the late afternoon haze that so often hangs over Los Angeles. Those spectacular acid-soaked sunsets must have been an inspiration to post-bop pianist LaMont Johnson. With the Pacific breeze blowing the NYC grime out of his 'fro, he set out to create an effervescent mixture of popular R&B and new-age gospel. He gathered some fly kids from around the way, in the hopes that their sugary harmonies would mask the corrosion that was already eating away at the age of groovy vibes. But real, deep funk is something that is lived in and worn out. It can't have an ideal pasted onto it like a cheesy bumper sticker. And the record suffered from the sun-soaked, soapbox idealism that was in vogue at the time, as well as vocals caught between the grit of James Brown and the polish of the 5th Dimension. The liner notes ask us to "Dig them. Dig their music." But Lamont forgot that, just like the sun, the funk always rises.

As much as Johnson wanted to turn away from the chaotic madness of his avant-garde past, funky jazz ran through his veins, and, when he got down to some bloodletting, he stopped talking *about* soul and shared his with us. The psychedelic Stax sound of "Maybe" opens with a simple keyboard riff. The bluesy funk gives Mokie (aka Monica), J.J. (aka Michael), and R.O.B. (aka Larry) a chance to let go with some gutsy singing. The pleading love song builds to a climax where the now-pounding piano locks in to the tight, swingin' horn section before releasing the kids to a breathless chorus of "Give it to me!"

Artist: Mokie, J.J. & R.O.B.
Record: *Speed of Light*
Label: Sun, Moon & Stars Records (SMS 7201s)
Release: 1972

The gem of this LP is the lost modern-soul classic, "Beverly." The arrangement, by Johnson and Gordon Konkle, comes off like Charlie Mingus getting spiritual during a boogie night in Tunisia. After a few bars of a walking bass line with conga, the track opens up to a laid-back groove. R.O.B. sounds tender and tough, as a slinky hi-hat propels us over a proto-disco bridge. It's during the spoken interlude that LaMont finally lets his hair down. He bangs out a masterful keyboard riff that nods to his days with Jackie McLean and Ornette Coleman, while predicting the freaked-out jazz funk of his future classics, *Sun, Moon and Stars* for Mainstream and *Nine* for the private Masterscores label. ◐ –*Robbie Busch*

Straight From the North
YO GOTTI AND THE NEW MEMPHIS SOUL

by Andria Lisle • photo by Justin Burks

Forty years after songsmith Isaac Hayes roamed the halls of Manassas High, North Memphis has become a breeding ground for the next generation of Southern soul, from Three 6 Mafia to the baby-faced rapper, Yo Gotti. Born Mario Mims and raised in the Ridge Crest Apartments complex—an insular ghetto overrun with pushers and pimps—Yo Gotti delivers his thuggish drawl through a mouthful of platinum, a trademark of the North-North. Fueled by a militant Swizzo beat and crafted at Ardent Studios, 2004's "Shawty" catapulted Gotti from the streets to a solo deal with TVT and a production deal with Cash Money, while his battle cries "Full Time" and "Dirty South Soldiers" helped to define Memphis's now sound.

You made your reputation off your first record, *Youngster on the Come Up*, an underground tape that you hustled on the streets. When did you know you wanted to rap?
On the streets, I was just hustling whatever, but I always did rap. Anyone who can rap or sing, I say they're born with that talent. Nobody taught me nothing hands on—I credit my street sense. I learned by making mistakes, by letting somebody get over on me. I paid for my lessons. I was always rapping around the neighborhood or at my school, but I didn't take it serious until the first time I got a check from it.

That was for your second album, *From the Dope Game to the Rap Game*?
Yeah, [Memphis-based indie distributor] Select-O-Hits gave me my first check, for $6500.

Was it a difficult transition, switching from the streets to the recording studio?
The rap game is a lot like the street game, as far as your hustle. Most of it is common sense: acting on the thought and the situation that's right in front of you. Hustling is like that too—you just have to deal with more people. Everybody wants to say they're "street," they're gangstas. According to all the rappers and all the managers, everybody's street, but the truth is, ain't none of 'em street! When they get in a street situation, they're gonna show that they don't know how to handle a problem.

The new abum, *Back 2 Da Basics*, has producers DJ Thoomp, Mannie Fresh, Carlos Broady, and Street Tunes.
Don't forget Scott Storch! He produced "That's What They Made It Foe." The old producers like to work with you in the studio, which is cool, versus the young producers, who are always sending you the beats.

"Full Time" was featured in *Hustle & Flow*. What did you think of the movie?
It's good that it was shot down here, and I was glad to be a part of it. But I don't see nobody come from Hollywood and do Memphis one hundred percent perfect. We don't run around in no Caprice box Chevy with a bad paint job; we run around in Benzes. Our clubs don't look like no houses. Otherwise, I think they got Memphis across.

The *New York Times* reviewed your last mixtape, *North Memphis Survivor*, and the new album. That's pretty high-profile stuff.
I heard about it, but it didn't mean nothing to me. ●

Memphis Underground
TAPE HUSTLERS ON THE COME-UP

by Andria Lisle • photo by Justin Burks

Craig Brewer's *Hustle & Flow*, released last summer, introduced the world to the Memphis rap scene via a nerdy White beat maker, a henpecked, would-be producer, and a rapping pimp. The movie gave us those unlikely heroes and told us that "Everybody's got to have a dream," a mantra that's already been realized by Three 6 Mafia, Al Kapone, 8Ball and MJG, and Yo Gotti. ¶ But if you believe that's all the Bluff City has to offer, think again. To find the city's best underground mixtapes and CDs, you'll have to bypass the brand-new Tower Records outlet downtown and head north to Ike's Record Shop, located in the Bay, or drive south to Boss Ugly Bob's, humbly located in the shadow of the Stax Museum of American Soul Music on South McLemore Avenue. ¶ If you want to find out what's really happening, cruise over to 2575 Lamar Avenue, the empty lot that was once Pressure World, the detail shop/car wash immortalized on Three 6 Mafia's "Don't Cha Get Mad." Watch the ashes—despite the fact that a blaze destroyed the big pink car wash this spring, the site is still a gathering spot for the city's burgeoning underground scene.

1. Criminal Manne "Stallion"
Two full years since "Tryna Bust Sumthing" exploded on local radio, this South Memphis underground tape king, who moves more than a thousand units a week, is still working the streets. "You gotta feed the underground. Niggas wanna turn on the radio and hear some shit that's straight gangsta, right from the hood," he explains. "Nobody wants to hear [Boogie Down Productions'] 'Stop the Violence' or any of that shit. Everybody wants to get crunk! They wanna hear, 'I'm gonna bust your motherfuckin' head!'"

2. Miscellaneous "Memphis Walk"
A brilliant update of "Land of 1,000 Dances," written by Miscellaneous and co-opted by Yo Gotti for *I Told U So*, his brand-new mixtape collaboration with DJ Drama. Check out the brilliant intro: "In A-Town, they got the A-Town Stomp, ya know!/ In St. Louis, they got the Chicken Head 'right thurr'/ Fat Joe, he got the Lean Back/ We're going to the right, over to the left, now back and forth like you do the two-step/ Memphis Walk/ Hey! Hey!/ Now Memphis Walk."

3. Mac E "I'm on Dat"
After ending a well-publicized feud with Yo Gotti in 2004, Mac E, aka Da Nu Boi, was flying high with "Got Deals." His latest joint, "I'm on Dat," is a collaboration with Orange Mound heavy MJG. The gloriously old school Memphis track (the lyrics are a litany of available drugs, while the music sounds like it might've been created on D'Jay's Casio) is just a preview of Mac E's highly anticipated third album, due on MJG Records this summer.

4. Nasty Nardo "Take a Picture"
Over the last decade, Nardo has represented the south side with songs like "Shake Joint," "Bitch Move," and his most recent local hit, "Don't Watch Me, Watch TV," which features Yung Kee. "I had to go out and bust my ass in the street with those songs, break 'em in the clubs," says Nardo. "'Take a Picture' is my way of saying, 'Look at me now, motherfuckers!' And for the first time, radio accepted a single from me without question."

5. Tom Skeemask "Jump Like U Want Sum"
This California-born, Orange Mound–raised rapper has released dozens of mixtapes and five full-length albums, collaborating with heavy hitters like Al Kapone, DJ Squeezy, and rising stars like Chopper Girl and DJ Zirk. "Jump Like U Want Sum" is true Memphis—a sound that, says Skeemask, can be stolen but never duplicated. "I ain't gonna sugarcoat it, man," he laments. "Memphis has been overlooked for years—all we can do is keep our heads up and keep moving."

So affordable you can give them away.

1,000 CDs IN JACKETS JUST 99¢ EACH!

SAVE $25

Download your coupon at
www.discmakers.com/wax

Perfect for singles, EPs, or full-length albums, CDs in jackets really pack a wallop. They're like those cool LP jackets, just smaller. Plus, they're ready in just 12 days and so unbelievably affordable, you could give them away. Not that you need to. Our jackets look so great you can sell them at full price any day. That's because we're the only place that throws in high-gloss UV coating for FREE with every jacket order – a $200 value! What else do we throw in? All our exclusive promotional tools, like six months' free web hosting, free online distribution, a free UPC bar code, a review from TAXI, and much more. So, if you're looking to save money on CDs without sacrificing quality, there's no better deal than CDs in jackets from Disc Makers. You can take that to the bank.

DISC MAKERS®
CD AND DVD MANUFACTURING MADE EASY

FREE CATALOG! Call 1-866-778-6101 or visit www.discmakers.com/wax

Clothing the Sound
Ronald Clyne (1925–2006)
by Dante Carfagna

Though visual designer Ronald Clyne might not be recognized by name alone, record collectors and graphics hounds will surely be familiar with his nearly autonomous body of work. Single-handedly developing the design ethos for Moses Asch's Folkways Records, Clyne used an economy of text and image to create album covers that are in turn stark, sublime, and instantly recognizable. Creating over five hundred jackets throughout the entirety of the Folkways tenure, Clyne is largely an unsung hero, chiefly due to the label's proletariat aspirations and lack of popular distribution. Usually limited to two colors and a single black-and-white photo, the designer made mountains out of molehills, often injecting ethnic recordings with a dose of familiarity or adding mystery to seemingly banal releases dealing with handwriting analysis, the sound of the dolphin, or the crying language of infants.

Throughout most of his life, Ronald Clyne was employed by the business of the printed word, designing dust jackets for books in nearly every genre for a variety of publishing houses. His earliest work can be found gracing the covers of many obscure volumes published in the 1940s by Arkham House, an imprint known for its rare releases by H. P. Lovecraft and other masters of the macabre. Clyne took over the lion's share of Folkways design work sometime in the late '50s, inheriting a position formerly held by Irwin Rosenhouse. Where Rosenhouse would use his own paintings and drawings as source material, Clyne opted for public domain photographs and established font libraries. His simple motifs and wise color selections suited the contents of the Folkways catalog well, offering the prospective listener a certain precise ambiguity while steering clear of potential prejudicial imagery. Clyne's unique aesthetic was as sympathetic and important to Asch's Folkways vision as Reid Miles's groundbreaking graphic assemblages were to Alfred Lion's vaunted Blue Note label.

Clyne worked for Asch and Folkways until the label's demise (upon the great owner's death) in 1986. Consistency would seem to be Ronald Clyne's most endearing trait, for even small, seemingly irrelevant later releases on Folkways still held to the strict, clean visual code established by the designer in the early '60s. Just as the contents of your average Folkways record teems with a sometimes unknown but always palpable sense of importance, so too do Clyne's ocular testimonies impart a timeless and searching quality rarely found in simple design. With the passing of Ronald Clyne on February 26, the world lost not just another graphic designer, but the creator of an entire visual language that invited so many of us into an unknown world of sound.

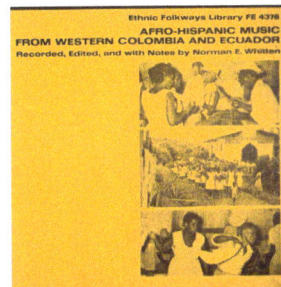

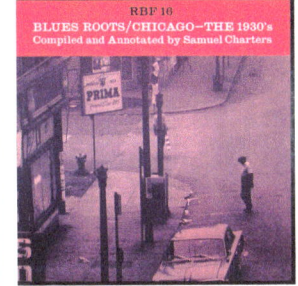

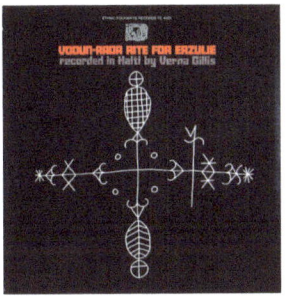
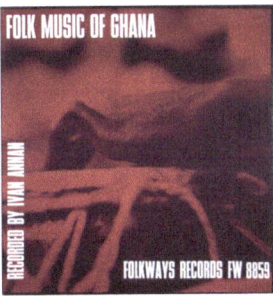

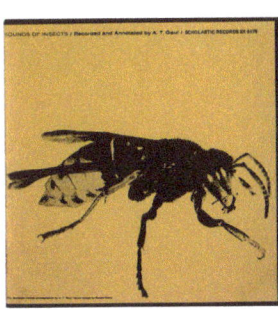

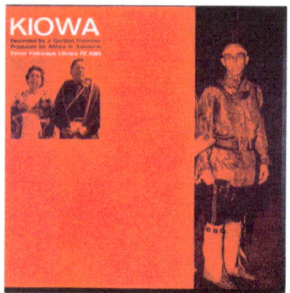

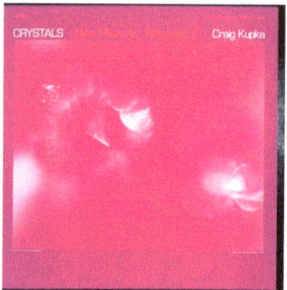

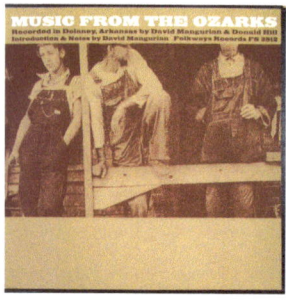

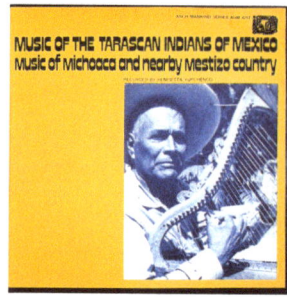

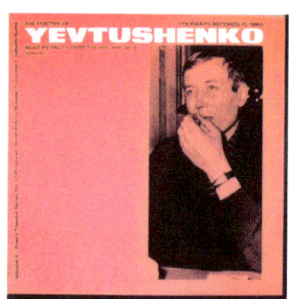

OH NO
EXODUS INTO UNHEARD RHYTHMS
PRODUCED BY OH NO.
FEAT. A.G. MURS POSDNUOS BUCKSHOT FRANK N DANK ROC 'C'
MADE WITH THE MUSIC OF GALT MACDERMOT
STONES THROW RECORDS WWW.STONESTHROW.COM

oh no "exodus into unheard rhythms" check the shit out   www.stonesthrow.com/ohno

THE CONNOISSEUR
BRAZILIAN MUSICIAN ED MOTTA HAS A TASTE FOR THE FINER SOUNDS IN LIFE

by Gareth Jones • photos by Jackson Bezerra

"Record collecting takes up ninety percent of my time." So says a man who has just released his eighth album and is currently writing a full onstage musical with actors, script, and all the trimmings. Needless to say, he must own a lot of records. Ed Motta is prolific not only in his musical knowledge and output but also in his hunger for information and originality. His love of fine wine, cuisine, and comics is well documented, but how many other musicians would describe a mood-changing album track as a "sorbet to clean the palate between courses"? His latest album, *Aystelum*, touches on free jazz and Broadway with a dance-floor banger thrown in for good measure. Across a scratchy telephone line to Rio, I was taken on a meandering journey that visited soul eccentricity and collecting culture with unexpected detours along the way.

Was music all around you when growing up?

Not especially at home. My parents were into European movies and literature, but there weren't too many records lying around. In the mid-'70s, when I was very young, I remember going to my uncle Tim Maia's concerts. This was during the period when he released his *Racional* albums. When he joined the religious group Universo em Desencanto around the same time, he gave his record collection to my mother, and she gave them to me! So my early listening was made up of soul, deep fatback funk, and orchestral music. East Harlem Bus Stop stands out.

You are a major pop artist in Brazil—how did that come about?

I had a big success with my first album *Ed Motta e Conexão Japeri* [Warner, 1988]. The band had been playing covers of songs by B.T. Express, the Crusaders, and the Blackbyrds to sold-out crowds in Rio and São Paulo before we got a record deal. Rock and post-punk was dominant, but we reissued the era of the Fender Rhodes, Black Rio, and the sound of Brass Construction. There was a big response to the sound and my solo career followed on from there.

Really, I have two different audiences: ten thousand people will come to my pop concerts in Brazil, but they don't like the collector-type music on recent albums like *Dwitza* [Universal/Whatmusic, 2002] and *Aystelum* [Trama/Ether Records, 2006]. These records have had a specific appeal overseas. Musically though, I see a line connecting both 1980s commercial pop and the Art Ensemble of Chicago. I wanted to do them all, as I'm fascinated in all the processes involved in making these supposedly unconnected artforms.

Is that what influenced you to move into more diverse and avant-garde music?

My third album *Entre e Ouca* [Warner, 1992] was my first jazz-influenced record, but it was a commercial disaster in Brazil. When I negotiated my contract with Universal, instead of cash advances, I wanted the freedom to make uncompromising music and follow my curiosity across a whole range of styles. To be honest, I don't enjoy being in a typical band situation. I prefer to work alone like a classical composer and always had a 4-track at home to record ideas. I've been quite hermetic in the past and used to spend three weeks at a time without leaving the house, studying cinema and learning different instruments. Producers in Brazil have a Phil Spector–like dominance over artists, but I've always produced my own albums. Leroy Hutson and Prince self-produced, so I took on the philosophy that a strong artist must do everything. [*laughs*] I wanted to be Prince!

Do you find the writing and recording process harder as a result, or is it simply more enjoyable?

Well, nothing worthwhile is ever easy, but the Broadway musical suite on *Aystelum* was the most complicated track I've mixed in my life so far! It's wonderful now but it proved to be a nightmare and took almost a week to finish. These songs will form a part of a complete musical that I'm writing at the moment.

On my solo projects, I have a paranoiac way of working in the studio: no-one is allowed in when I'm not there; no one can bring friends round to hang out, and there is no chitchat during the session—it's a very military approach! [My sound engineer] Duda Mello is my Roger Nichols [who was Steely Dan's engineer extraordinaire]. If I was a millionaire, I would pay him not to work with anyone else! I'm interested in the mystique of the studio like Rudy Van Gelder when he recorded for Prestige, Blue Note, and Riverside. At the end of a session, he would put a blanket over the microphones so nobody would know which mic he'd used to get a certain sound from a particular instrument.

How did your interest in vintage synthesizers begin?

First of all, I always use an analog synth sound. I enjoy the perfection and imperfection of them—the imperfections give style! The keyboard player in my first band was into old equipment, and in the mid-'80s, relatively speaking, they were very cheap—you could pick up a Wurlitzer for $200. I have three Wurlitzers, two Rhodes, and two Clavinets. It all fits into the nerd/collector aspect of my personality. Everybody uses Rhodes these days as an obvious way to convey emotion, but my current favorite is the RMI piano. It was the first electronic keyboard—*not* electro-acoustic—and was very cheap when it originally came out. Sun Ra played it a lot in the 1970s, and Miles asked Keith Jarrett to use it. Herbie Hancock also used it on Miles's "Filles de Kilimajaro." Most tracks on *Aystelum* feature the RMI. It has no nuances or dynamics—it's at full level all the time, but it does have an expressive, nostalgic sound.

RECORD RUNDOWN

Marku Marku Ribas (Underground) 1976

Marku's second album is wild, raw soul with a Brazilian influence and dirty Clavinet! This is the best arrangement that João Donato ever made in his life. I remember it being a big record at Dingwalls in Camden when I visited London in 1992. DJ Mitch, who I became friends with, had a copy, and I looked at Brazilian music differently from that point onwards. Marku's voice is very strong here, with traces of Leon Thomas and John Lucien in his scatting. The album was also released in France with French lyrics, but that's extremely rare—I think Cliffy has a copy!

Freedom of Speech Billy Parker's Fourth World (Strata East) 1975

I'm a fanatic of Strata East and turned to eBay to complete my collection of the entire back catalogue. This is one of the first records to feature Dee Dee Bridgewater and the Bridgewater Brothers Cecil and Ronald on trumpet and sax respectively. The feel is spiritual jazz and soul and there are even samba influences present. "Get with It" is one of my ten favorite tracks of all time, and this album, along with the label as a whole, has had a big influence on my music. The ambience of Strata East is very strong and distinct—a unique mixture of intellect, politics, and spiritualism.

Copacabana Sadia Junior Mendes (RCA) 1982

This was produced by Robson and Lincoln—Brazil's answer to the Mizell Brothers. They were prolific producers and arrangers during the 1970s. Tim Maia worked with them, and I visited some of the sessions at their studios as a child. It's a great favorite of mine—a funky and sophisticated record with harp strings and synthesizers. There's a "Bobby Caldwell" funkiness to the cover! The only album he ever recorded as an artist—Junior Mendes is now a producer.

Al Rahman! Cry of the Floridian Tropic Son Abdul Rahim Ibrahim (formerly Doug Carn) (Tablichi) 1977

A very rare and expensive record. It's different to the style of his Black Jazz [Records] albums and was made in 1977, but there's nothing related to disco on here. Instead, there are lots of analogue synths alongside lyrical themes of spirituality and Black consciousness. He sings for the first time on this record as he was no longer with Jean Carn, who had appeared on his earlier work. I discovered this kind of music after listening to Norman Connors. In the '70s, Brazilian soap operas used Norman Connors songs as theme music—another tune I remember was "Papaya" by Ursula Dudziak (Arista 7-inch, 1975). I was seven years old at the time, and these songs inspired me to scat for the rest of my life.

A Little Night Music Stephen Sondheim (Columbia) 1973

I love Broadway musicals. Sondheim is one of my favorite composers from *any* style of music. It was a big influence not only on *Aystelum* but also on *Dwitza*. This album sounds like a dream. God is listening to "A Little Night Music," and I pray before Stephen Sondheim! It is compositionally perfect and its lyrics are wonderful chronicles about society and the individual, dealt with in a literary and stylish way. The way Sondheim constructs these songs is strongly linked to the narrative of the musical. "Liaisons" is one of my favorite tracks—I find the strength and respect that old singers can bring to a piece beautiful.

Shoyo Jurin Yoshiaki Fujikawa and East Asia Orchestra (Mobys) 1984

This relates to my mania for Japan and Japanese jazz, of which I have a big collection. Their way of jazz is in a similar vein to Strata East and I love the way they do it. Fujikawa is a sax player, influenced by Sun Ra as well as Strata. Some people wrongly assume that Japanese jazz will be just an imitation of the Western style, but it is very deep in its own right. This record is very rare in Japan itself—I bought it in Fukuoka, and that day I had the best sushi in my life!

Bajo Belgrano Spinetta Jade (Raton Finta) 1983

Luis Alberto Spinetta and his jazz-fusion years, which came after an inventive time with a psych-prog band he formed, called Invisible, in the mid-'70s. I love Argentina and its music—many Brazilian artists play in Argentina but not vice versa. As a Steely Dan fanatic, I see Spinetta as the South American Donald Fagen. Like Fagen, he constructs complex harmonies and changes, combined with acid, sarcastic lyrics. He's also a great guitar player. There is a typically early '80s feel to this album and a Weather Report style of fusion—people don't seem to pay much attention to this type of sound. Jazz fusion in Argentina can be traced back to the 1950s and '60s with artists such as Jorge Lopez Ruiz and Horacio "Chivo" Borraro. Spinetta is my favorite South American pop artist.

Desbunde Total Johnny Alf (Chantecler) 1978

If Billy Strayhorn experienced work with a Clavinet, it might have sounded like this. Johnny Alf is a Brazilian composer, singer, and pianist. He's my favorite Brazilian singer ever and a very underrated artist. A rarity in his career—this is a very funky album. He was more associated with traditional ballads and made his name in the 1950s and '60s, constructing songs with intros and verses in the style of Broadway musicals. This was a new departure and a different sound marked by synthesizers and funky Clavinet playing. He never made a record like it again.

Another Sleeper Max Middleton and Robert Ahwai (Harvest Fusion) 1979

The sound quality here, together with EMT turntables, makes me cry! I play the Fender Rhodes because of Max Middleton. One of my big moments of 2005 was to meet

Max in the studio when I invited him to play on the *Jazzinho* album I was producing in London. He has *the* best Rhodes sound for me, as well as being one of the greatest Clavinet players I've ever heard. I listened to this record a lot when I was still at school and heard him play on Jeff Beck's jazz-fusion albums of the mid-'70s. There is something about the timbre of his Rhodes with which he makes the instrument his own, and it's a very special record for me. An early influence before I had decided to *make* music and was planning to open a record store!

Aja Steely Dan (ABC Records) 1977

When I work in other studios than my own, or a place that I don't know the control-room sound exactly, I must listen to *Aja* several times. It's my favorite record out of my entire collection. It might sound like an obvious choice, but the album has given me inspiration in a very personal way. For me, Steely Dan is the most perfect thing I ever heard in my life—it is a religion! The sound quality, solos, and musicians are flawless on this record—they had reached their high point. They used to take more than a week to mix one track, so it's expensive to be influenced by their studio habits! I'm living in these days of laptops and lack of money, but I love the exaggerated way of life from that era: "Please, send me another grand piano—this one's no good!" I'm a fan and I have a very emotional response to any of their work, including Donald Fagen's solo albums. I collect jazz, studied harmony, and learnt the piano because of Steely Dan.

Gareth Jones *lives in London where he's currently searching for SADiE.*

Aystelum by Ed Motta is out now on Ether Records (ethermusic.net).

INSPIRATION

PERSONALIZATION

2007 Scion tC
Starting at $16,940*
Standard features include

Six-speaker Pioneer CD stereo • Steering-wheel audio controls • iPod® and MP3 player capable • Satellite radio ready • Panorama moonroof • 17" alloy wheels • Cruise control • 5-year, 60,000-mile Powertrain warranty†

*MSRP includes delivery, processing, and handling fee; excludes taxes, title, license, and optional equipment. Dealer price may vary. †See your local Scion dealer for additional details on the Scion limited warranty. Functioning satellite radio requires satellite radio compatibility, receiver and satellite monthly service fee. See your local Scion dealer for further details. © 2006 Toyota Motor Sales, USA, Inc. Scion and the Scion logo are trademarks of Toyota Motor Corporation, and Toyota is a registered trademark of Toyota Motor Corporation. For more information, call 1-866-70-SCION (1-866-707-2466), or visit scion.com. iPod is a registered trademark of Apple Computer, Inc. Apple is not a participant in or sponsor of this promotion.

REALIZATION

Vehicle is for show only and not street legal; modified with non-Genuine Scion parts (which void the warranty and may adversely impact performance).

Customization accessories include

Fog light kit • Ground-effects kit • Rear-lip spoiler • Sport pedal covers • Shift knobs • Interior light kit • EMX Super-7 18" alloy wheels • TRD performance exhaust • Yakima roof rack • Billet oil-filler cap

18" Alloy Wheels

Sport Pedal Covers

Shift Knobs

Rear-lip Spoiler

what moves you
scion.com

FUNK USED TO BE A BAD WORD
A PARLIAMENT-FUNKADELIC PRIMER

by Matt Rogers • models by Jean-Yves Blanc • illustration by Alberto Forero

"Once upon a time called Right Now"

Over the years, much ink has been spilled regarding George Clinton and the controversial history of Parliament-Funkadelic. So, you ask, why waste any more on the, perhaps, tired topic? Well, a few reasons: 1. Despite being inducted into the Rock and Roll Hall of Fame in 1997, as well as being the most sampled musical collective on the planet, and when considering the evolution, breadth, and impact of their fifty-year run of recorded musical output—from doo-wop to hip-hop, literally[1]—as well as their visual, iconic reach beyond popular music, Parliament-Funkadelic are *still* not given the props they deserve. 2. Though he is undoubtedly a shrewd mack daddy, songwriter, and producer, George Clinton would *clearly* not have achieved such success and fame without the incredible contributions of *scores* of musicians, arrangers, artists, and average Joes; yet folks always seem to go to Clinton for "the story." 3. Afro-nauts in a spaceship?

"Funk used to be a bad word"

Long before they were Afro-nauts on a spaceship, the Parliaments were Afro-nots in a barbershop. There are no Funkadelics yet. Hell, there isn't even a Sputnik, let alone a Mothership. And the only cloning going on is the replication of the flyest finger wave on the next customer's head. It's true; what becomes the most funked-out musical empire ever whiffed starts out with a handful of dudes processing hair in a New Jersey ghetto. Yes, they *are* singers, but the bread comes from how many asses they can keep still in the barber chair, not shake on the dance floor.

"If you will suck my soul, I will lick your funky emotions"

The Parliaments were spearheaded fifty years ago by one teenaged George Clinton in Newark, New Jersey. Southern-born and Northern-raised, this eldest of nine is inspired by the vocal harmonizing of the secular and the sacred. Today kids rap; back then, they sang. The Parliaments go on to record a few 45s and, chasing the Temptations and Four Tops, even have a failed Motown audition in '62. It's around this time that the "original" Parliaments lineup is solidified, consisting of George, Grady Thomas, Calvin Simon, Clarence "Fuzzy" Haskins, and Raymond Davis. Most of them work together in a Plainfield barbershop—the Black Soap Palace—processing hair and making demo tapes which George, being the business face of the group, routinely shops around on his weekend trips to the soul capitol of the world: Detroit. At the same time, the group hones its songwriting skills in the Brill building in New York City, and its performance game locally: "We called it the chitlin circuit, playing those bars back in the woods," recounts Fuzzy. "You only had—maybe—a keyboard player with you, a guitar player; the amplifier was maybe as big as a footstool."

"The rich got a big piece of this and that/ The poor got a big piece of roaches and rats/ Can you get to that?"

In 1966, the Parliaments begin recording for Revilot Records. In the spring of '67, one of their songs, "(I Wanna) Testify," becomes a pop hit, and suddenly they find themselves headlining the Apollo Theater and revving up for a tour. Lacking a backup band, they enlist Plainfield native and barbershop employee Billy Nelson, a sixteen-year-old guitarist who eventually switches to bass and recruits Eddie Hazel (lead guitar), Ramon "Tiki" Fulwood (drums), then later Tawl Ross (rhythm guitar) and Bernie Worrell (keys).[2] Billy christens this younger "backup" band Funkadelic, who, influenced by bands such as the Beatles, Sly and the Family Stone, Jimi Hendrix, and Vanilla Fudge, will greatly impact the elder Parliaments, replacing the aesthetic of Motown for that of a hippified psychedelic rock.

"Behold. I am Funkadelic. I am not of your world but fear me not."

After the success of "Testify," the Parliaments become embroiled in the first of many future lawsuits, and are prevented from finishing their debut album (tentatively titled *Testify* or *All Your Goodies are Gone*). This leads to George signing Funkadelic to Detroit's newly minted Westbound Records, a stroke of genius, for it allows (what is now) Parliafunkadelicment Thang Inc. to motor on. And this is usually where much of the confusion begins. Parliament (the "s" was later dropped) is essentially the vocalists; Funkadelic is

JULY 22, 1940
George Clinton is born in an outhouse in Kannapolis, North Carolina.

1955–56
George Clinton forms the Parliaments with fellow classmates at Clinton Place Junior High School in Plainfield, New Jersey.

1956
Grady Thomas joins the group.

1957
Calvin Simon joins the group from the Crystals.

1958
Parliaments record "Poor Willie" b/w "Party Boys" for Hull Records.

1959
"Poor Willie" re-released on APT (ABC-Paramount).

PARLIAMENT-FUNKADELIC

1967
"(I Wanna) Testify" enters the R&B singles chart, hitting #3, and also rises to #20 on the Pop Top Forty. ★ Record several other singles for the label, including a cover of "Sgt. Pepper's Lonely Hearts Club Band" for an intended full-album Parliaments release. ★ The Parliaments tour. Billy "Bass" Nelson then gets Eddie Hazel and Ramon "Tiki" Fulwood to join what becomes known as Funkadelic. ★ Funkadelic uses Vanilla Fudge's equipment, discover the heavy sound they've been seeking.

1968
Calvin Simon returns from Vietnam. ★ Holding company Parliafunkadelicment Thang, Inc. is formed by Parliaments. ★ Legal disputes with Revilot and Motown arise. Parliaments stop recording. ★ George Clinton and Funkadelic sign with Westbound Records. ★ Billy, Eddie, and Tiki quit for the first time.

1969
Funkadelic regroups as Tawl Ross and Bernie Worrell are enlisted. ★ Funkadelic records first album, *Funkadelic*, for Westbound, released in 1970.

1970
Funkadelic releases *Free Your Mind...And Your Ass Will Follow* (Westbound). ★ Parliaments drop the "s." ★ First album by Parliament, *Osmium*, is released on Holland-Dozier-Holland's Invictus Records.

1971
Funkadelic releases *Maggot Brain* (Westbound). ★ Original Funkadelic members quit. Tawl Ross incapacitated by drug trip. ★ Tyrone Lampkin becomes drummer.

1972
William "Bootsy" and Phelps "Catfish" Collins, Frankie "Kash" Waddy, Garry Shider, and Cordell "Boogie" Mosson join the fold. ★ Funkadelic releases double-LP *America Eats Its Young* (Westbound). ★ Artist Pedro Bell joins.

1979
Bootsy's Rubber Band releases *This Boot Is Made for Fonk-n* (Warner Brothers). ★ Funkadelic releases *Uncle Jam Wants You* (Warner Brothers). It goes gold. "(Not Just) Knee Deep" goes #1. ★ Parliament releases *Gloryhallastoopid (Or Pin the Tale on the Funky)* (Casablanca). It goes gold. ★ Parlet releases *Invasion of the Booty Snatchers* (Casablanca). ★ The Brides of Funkenstein releases *Funk or Walk* (Atlantic).

1980
Bootsy releases *Ultra Wave* (Warner Brothers). ★ The Brides of Funkenstein release *Never Buy Texas From a Cowboy* (Atlantic). ★ The Sweat Band, a splinter group of Bootsy's Rubber Band, releases debut on George Clinton's short-lived Uncle Jam Records. ★ Parlet releases *Play Me or Trade Me* (Casablanca). ★ Bootsy produces Zapp's self-titled debut, which goes #1. ★ Parliament releases *Trombipulation* (Casablanca).

1981
Funkadelic releases *The Electric Spanking of War Babies* (Warner Brothers).

1982
George Clinton releases first solo album, *Computer Games*, on Capitol Records. "Atomic Dog" goes #1. ★ Bootsy releases *The One Giveth, the Count Taketh Away* (Warner Brothers).

1983
George Clinton releases *You Shouldn't-Nuf Bit Fish* (Capitol). ★ P-Funk All-Stars release *Urban Dancefloor Guerrillas* on Uncle Jam/CBS Associated Records.

1989
Producer Prince Paul samples Funkadelic's "Knee Deep" (from *Uncle Jam Wants You*) for "Me, Myself, and I" for De La Soul's debut album, *3 Feet High and Rising*. ★ George Clinton releases *The Cinderella Theory* on Prince's Paisley Park/Warner Brothers Records. ★ P-Funk starts touring heavily again.

1960
Clarence "Fuzzy" Haskins joins the group from the Bel-Aires.

SEPT. 1962
Failed audition at Motown. Ray Davis joins the group from the Del Larks.

1963
George Clinton signs publishing deal w/ Motown's Jobete Publishing.

1964
Parliaments record demos for Motown, a few of which are later recorded by the Jackson Five and the Supremes.

1965
Parliaments release "Heart Trouble" b/w "That Was My Girl" on Golden World Records.

1966
Parliaments sign with Revilot Records and record "(I Wanna) Testify" and "I Can Feel the Ice Melting" ★ Billy Nelson recruited to play rhythm guitar.

SELECTED TIMELINE

1973
Funkadelic releases *Cosmic Slop* (Westbound).

1974
Funkadelic releases *Standing on the Verge of Getting It On* (Westbound). ★ Parliament releases *Up for the Down Stroke* on Casablanca Records. ★ Gary "Mudbone" Cooper joins.

1975
Funkadelic releases *Let's Take It to the Stage* (Westbound). ★ Funkadelic releases *Funkadelic's Greatest Hits* (Westbound). ★ Parliament releases *Chocolate City* (Casablanca). ★ Glenn Goins and Jerome "Bigfoot" Brailey join.

1976
Fred Wesley and Maceo Parker join the fold, as well as Michael Hampton. ★ Parliament releases *Mothership Connection* (Casablanca). It goes platinum. ★ Bootsy's Rubber Band releases *Stretchin' Out in Bootsy's Rubber Band* on Warner Brothers. ★ Funkadelic releases *Hardcore Jollies* on Warner Brothers. ★ Funkadelic releases *Tales of Kidd Funkadelic* (Westbound). ★ Parliament releases *The Clones of Dr. Funkenstein* (Casablanca). It goes gold. ★ Fuzzy Haskins releases *A Whole Nother Thang* (Westbound). ★ Tiki Fulwood dies. ★ The legendary Mothership Tour takes off.

1977
Bootsy's Rubber Band releases *Ahh...The Name Is Bootsy, Baby!* (Warner Brothers). It goes gold. ★ Funkadelic releases *The Best of the Funkadelic Early Years* (Westbound). ★ Parliament releases *Funkentelechy vs. the Placebo Syndrome* (Casablanca). It goes platinum. ★ Sir Nose D'Voidoffunk is born. ★ "Flash Light," with its Moog bass line, goes #1. ★ Parliament releases *Parliament Live: P-Funk Earth Tour* (Casablanca). ★ Fred Wesley and the Horny Horns release *A Blow for Me, a Toot to You* on Atlantic Records. ★ Eddie Hazel releases *Games, Dames, and Guitar Thangs* on Warner Brothers.

1978
Walter "Junie" Morrison joins the collective. ★ Bootsy's Rubber Band releases *Bootsy? Player of the Year* (Warner Brothers). "Bootzilla" goes #1. ★ Funkadelic releases *One Nation Under a Groove* (Warner Brothers). It goes platinum. "One Nation Under a Groove" goes #1. ★ Parliament releases *Motor-Booty Affair* (Casablanca). It goes gold. "Aqua Boogie" goes #1. ★

Quazar, a Plainsfield, NJ, band created by Kevin Goins, brother of P-Funker Glen Goins, releases *Quazar* on Arista Records. ★ After quitting P-Funk, Glen Goins helped Quazar, but dies before the record is complete. ★ Bernie Worrell releases *All the Woo in the World* (Arista). ★ Fuzzy Haskins releases *Radio Active* (Westbound). ★ Parlet releases *Pleasure Principle* on Casablanca. ★ Original Parliaments members Calvin Simon, Fuzzy Haskins, and Grady Thomas leave the group.

1990
For their debut album *Sex Packets*, Digital Underground samples heavily from the P-Funk catalog ("Flash Light," "Aqua Boogie," "Motor-Booty Affair," "Let's Play House," "Atomic Dog"), helping to spark the West Coast trend of sampling P-Funk. ★ P-Funk All-Stars release *Live at the Beverly Theater in Hollywood* (Westbound Records).

1992
For his multiplatinum solo debut, *The Chronic*, Dr. Dre borrows (and interpolates) P-Funk hooks, loops, and synth stylings to create what is now known as the West Coast (and/or gangsta) rap sound (though others had sampled P-Funk well before this release). Dr. Dre acknowledges P-Funk by calling his sound G-funk, and sports a Funkadelic *Maggot Brain* T-shirt in his video to "Dre Day," helping to reignite the public's interest in the band. ★ George Clinton and the P-Funk All-Stars release *Go Fer Your Funk George Clinton Family Series Volume One* on AEM Records. ★ Funkadelic releases *Music for Your Mother* (AEM Records). ★ Eddie Hazel dies.

1993
Continuing to boost P-Funk's popularity among the younger generation, Dr. Dre produced Snoop Dog's debut, borrowing from Funkadelic's "Knee Deep" and Clinton's "Atomic Dog" to craft hit songs.

1997
Parliament-Funkadelic is inducted into Rock and Roll Hall of Fame.

2005
Ray Davis dies.

2006
Wax Poetics publishes the P-Funk issue.

essentially the band (though nearly everyone in Funkadelic also sings lead), but the two groups are the same cast. Parliament sings on Funkadelic records and vice versa; a practice that continues until their demise. It is also the same touring unit, whether under the banner of Parliament, Funkadelic, or Parliafunkadelicment. Whatever the moniker, the group puts on a notoriously in-your-face live show, both on the chitlin circuit and in the predominantly White hard-rock scene, during a time when race riots erupt and a common sound within a club is the click of a pistol's hammer being cocked. The Funkadelics themselves survive three shoot-outs. After seeing a Funkadelic show, former Parliaments' rival Sammy Campbell of the Del Larks could hardly believe the group's transformation from Temptations wannabes: "George had a show! One night at the Apollo, he dropped that robe and looked like he was buck naked. I think he had a bodysuit on that looked like his skin. Oh, it was dynamite. The girls, they just freaked the fuck out, man. They bugged out. I looked at him and freaked out myself, thinking, 'What the *fuck* is wrong with George?' The band was like, 'Fuck it.'"

"Free your mind and your ass will follow/ the kingdom of heaven is within"

Toward the end of '71, however, drugs, power struggles, and issues with money cause the original Funkadelics to bolt (though Bernie, Eddie, and Tiki would return)—after recording three highly original yet only moderately successful albums—thus beginning a new phase in the life of P-Funk. Two years in the making, the release of Funkadelic's double LP *America Eats Its Young*, replete with horns, strings, and a political bent, is a turning point, and showcases the contributions of dozens of musicians—notably J.B. alums Bootsy and Phelps Collins, as well as Plainfield natives Garry Shider and Cordell Mosson—and illustrates Clinton's growth as a producer and Worrell's as an arranger. Clinton then strikes a deal for Parliament with Neil Bogart's Casablanca Records, thus setting in motion the unprecedented move of having essentially the same band, Parliament-Funkadelic, record simultaneously for two different labels.[3]

"Soul is a ham hock in your cornflakes"

His business savvy established, Clinton focuses on truly commercializing funk on a massive scale, incorporating James Brown's notion of "the One" that had been brought in by Bootsy, and then later by Maceo Parker and Fred Wesley in '76 for the *Mothership Connection*. Moreover, he begins to push (with the help of his entire posse) a sci-fi funk-laden iconography, mythology, and lexicon, complete with cartoonish characters like Dr. Funkenstein and Sir Nose D'voidoffunk, who reappear over the course of several albums. With James Brown, Sly Stone, and other major funk figures on the commercial decline, the public buys into the gimmicks big-time, and Parliament-Funkadelic bring their sci-fi funk opera—several-hundred-thousand-dollar flying spaceship and all—to sold-out arenas across the country (a far cry from the incarnation that used to sweat decibels with the likes of the MC5 and the Amboy Dukes a mere five years previous). Over the next several years, Clinton extends his reach by creating a P-Funk cottage industry, inking major-label deals for Bootsy's Rubber Band, the Brides of Funkenstein, Fred Wesley, Parlet, Eddie Hazel, and Bernie Worrell, and eventually creating his own record label: Uncle Jam.

"Put a glide in your stride and a dip in your hip and come on the Mothership"

As the commercial success skyrockets, however, not everyone is happy. The original Parliaments (except for Ray Davis) leave over money disputes in '78 just after One Nation Under a Groove goes platinum. It's a bitter ending that eventually catches up to Clinton by the end of the decade as drugs take their toll, lawsuits begin to fly, and the name Parliament-Funkadelic is lost. Though P-Funk would be resurrected in the '80s and start heavily touring again in the '90s, their newer recordings won't match the success of their funk heyday. The sampling, however, by the likes of Dr. Dre, De La Soul, Snoop Dogg, Digital Underground, OutKast, and countless others, as well as their impact on folks such as Rick James, Prince, Bad Brains, Fishbone, Living Colour, and Red Hot Chili Peppers, earthquake-proof their legacy.

"Light years in time…ahead of our time…"

The following pages are the words from those who wanted to tell a snippet of their P-Funksperience. We don't pretend to present any semblance of a final word (we sure as hell know we ain't giving you the first), as a forest of felled trees would be required to capture a Parliafunkadelicment Thang and all of its ramifications. *Buy* some of this music (much of which has recently been newly annotated and remastered), check out some of the other sources on the subject, and go support those P-Funk alums that are still taking it to the stage.

Furthermore, over the course of many, many moons, we attempted to contact as many of the men and women involved, past and present, with P-Funk in all of its incarnations. Several folks declined comment or could not be located. Others provided rich conversation (on and off the record). And for others, still, we simply ran out of time. To all those willing people we missed, we greatly apologize. Hopefully, there will be a next time. And to those who aren't among the living to tell their story, we thank you for your service to Uncle Jam's Army and dedicate this to your memory. Your music marches on.

There are many sources that provide a bit of P-Funk education. Here are a few:

The History of Funk by Rickey Vincent; newfunktimes.com; duke.edu/motherpage; *Music for your Mother* compilation liner notes by Rob Bowman; Greg Tate's "Doin' It in Your Earhole" liner notes to *Tear the Roof Off: 1974–1980* (Casablanca); 2005's *One Nation Under a Groove* P-Funk documentary; and soul-patrol.com.

"Something about the music, it got into my pants"

Notes

1. Speaking generally about P-Funk is, in the end, inane. Listen to their oeuvre as a whole and you will hear much of the history of popular music: gospel, doo-wop, R&B, soul, rock and roll, classical, psychedelic rock, heavy metal, punk, funk, disco, and hip-hop. Tracing that evolution, however, is, um, messy.
2. One cannot underestimate the importance of Bernie Worrell to the evolution and accomplishments of the P-Funk universe. A classically trained child prodigy, Bernie served as the anchor for many of the P-Funk projects, which allowed each incarnation to freak out, experiment, and always come, musically, home.
3. Generally speaking, while both "groups" feature premium gospel-tight vocals, Funkadelic, was more funk rock and guitar heavy, while Parliament, adorned with slick horn arrangements, was more funky R&B.

EL - PRODUCTO
"I'LL SLEEP WHEN YOU'RE DEAD"
DEFINITIVE JUX RECORDS

WWW.SCIFEN.COM

scifen
AVAILABLE ONLINE AT
digitalgravel.com

FROM DOO-WOP TO FUNKADELIA

CALVIN SIMON, GRADY THOMAS, AND FUZZY HASKINS OF THE PARLIAMENTS

by Matt Rogers • photos © Michael Ochs Archives.com

Amid all the controversy and fame, the psychedelic madness and Mothership mythos, it is perhaps somewhat understandable that the very foundation on which the Parliament-Funkadelic empire was built is so often lost within the glitter of platinum records: the vocals. In particular, the vocal harmonies. In fact, I defy you to think of any other band that has produced and procured more worthy singers and harmonizers, male or female, than this one. (Time's tickin', son). ¶ This P-Funk tradition, equal parts pop and gospel, was started by the original Parliaments—George Clinton, Grady Thomas, Calvin Simon, Clarence "Fuzzy" Haskins, and Raymond Davis—during an era when Frankie Lymon and the Teenagers were *the* Macks and Sam Cooke was becoming *the* Daddy. The Parliaments were vocal harmonizers, aka doo-woppers, to the core. Their voices were their instruments, and from the bottom to the top, top to the bottom, they were clean, tight, and knew how to process some hair. Hungry for musical fame outside the barbershop, they strove and struggled together throughout the '50s, '60s, and '70s, their inner ragged funkiness eventually leading the way to a Parliafunkadelicment type of thang. Success did indeed come. But in 1978, after much acrimony and perceived deceit, the original Parliaments (minus Ray) jumped from what had become George Clinton's ship (Grady would eventually return).

Twenty years later, the Parliaments (sans Clinton) reunited to form Original "P" Funk, from which an album and tour was born. For those of you who missed those initial shows, tsk-tsk, you missed a slab of the real deal. Sadly, bass singer extraordinaire Ray Davis passed last year. The Original "P," led by Fuzzy and Grady (and with Ray's son Derrick taking over the bass duties), continues to record and tour. Calvin Simon, despite retiring from the road, continues to hit the charts with his funkified solo gospel albums. He gleefully admits life is good: "I'm like a stag been put out to pasture. The only things I worry about today is: when's tee-off time and what outfit I'm gonna wear?" So let's hear from the stags themselves.

LITTLE OLD COUNTRY BOYS

CALVIN: We've been having chirpers in our family a long time. My father sang with the Dixie Hummingbirds and other gospel groups. When I was six, I was singing in the senior choir in church. Every Sunday at six P.M., we'd have a half-hour program on the radio; by the time I was eight, I was singing some leads. Bexley, West Virginia—that's where I grew up. Typical Southern town, family oriented, in the mountains. We had a very large family. When I was thirteen, we moved to New Jersey, and so when I was fourteen going on fifteen, I met George. He had come in from North Carolina; Raymond came in from South Carolina; Fuzzy came in from West Virginia; Grady's the only one born in New Jersey. [*laughs*]

GRADY: I'm from Newark. I grew up around the church but not *in* the church. My mother used to send me to Sunday school, and I used to be mad, but across the street from the church was a radio station. I used to sneak over in the morning and listen to all the gospel groups. One time it was the Soul Stirrers; I was so taken out! I knew I wanted to sing, but I didn't know it was gonna be the kind of music I ended up doin'.

FUZZY: I come up from West Virginia in 1955. My sister, Murray Haskins, she was like my mom. I never got a chance to spend any time with my mother; [she] passed when I was seven months old. I loved drums and rhythm; it was born in me. I would always sing and always bang on the table when

(*opposite*) The Parliaments, October 1966: (left to right) Ray Davis, Calvin Simon, Clarence "Fuzzy" Haskins, Grady Thomas, and George Clinton.

I was eating. We lived right by the railroad track. I would beat sounds to the train running across the tracks. I would keep time to that clicking of those wheels with my knife and fork, and my sister would smack me to shut up many a day. We'd also harmonize—she'd be cooking—we'd be singing spiritual songs.

GRADY: My father, Grady Thomas, was a great saxophonist. He disappeared on me when I was seven, eight years old. [He] used to take me to the clubs and sit me up on the counter, and that's possibly where I got the music influence too, 'cause he was so popular, travelin' around the country in a lot of those big groups, playing jazz and bebopping. I used to be crying, "I want my daddy!" Hey, as a matter of fact, he's still disappeared; I was never able to find him. I don't know if he's dead or alive right today. When I got older, I used to play conga drums in the park, playing pots and pans, congas—just start jamming—that's where I got my drumming inspiration. [Later] I used to go over to New York and really started liking that Puerto Rican music; going to the Palladium and watch them dance the mambo. I was around sixteen years old [when] I met George, 'cause he was processing hair in Newark, and somebody took me to some local yokel Parliaments thing. I was singing in a local group and he waved my hair in the back of a van. From there, that's how we got singing together.

FUZZY: In high school, our first singing group was called the V.J.s [Voice Jokers]. We used to wear these white shirts with a red sweater pulled over backwards, and a jacket, white collars sticking out. We won some little talent shows, but some of these guys got into drugs and overdosed, and a lot of guys just didn't want to sing but get attention from girls. We'd stand in the hallways singing, or at night under the lights in Potter's Crossing in the country, we'd sit, sing, and steal this guy's grapes till the wee hours of the morning. I failed a few subjects my junior year and they wouldn't let me play sports, so I got mad and quit school for a year. But my sister was slaving in the laundry to get me in school and buy me clothes—we were poor—and I thought about that, went back, and finished high school. [George] didn't have no driving license, and he and I started seeing some girls, Elaine and Vivian, over in Perth Amboy, New Jersey. I would give him a ride over there if he did my hair and sometimes give him a ride home to Newark from Plainfield. So we started being friends before I even got into the group.

CALVIN: In Jersey [in the '50s], on any night, on any given corner, you had people singing doo-wop. I was singing at the time in my own group, the Crystals. We were doing good. So we're doing this talent show at the Y, and George and his group were in the audience. My group won the show: $25 or something. I had a real high falsetto, and in the '50s, falsettos and bass singers, man, that was the theme of the year. So the next week, I went to get my hair done, 'cause I had a process at the time, and I heard about this guy that did hair well. I went to the Uptown Tonsorial Parlor on Springfield in Newark where George was working. He had a lineup of people in there doing hair, and everyone was talking. The barbershop was political heaven, man. If you wanted to find out what was happening in the community or the world, you went to the barbershop! So as George is doing my hair, he says, "Hey, I saw you singing." So we started harmonizing, and, oh man, we just hit it off! Next thing I know, I was in the group. Grady and I used to sing together in school. He's the one who told George about me. But then when he heard me sing—I can sing anything from baritone to falsetto to first tenor—Grady was out and I was in. And we were best friends!

GRADY: George fired me to get Calvin. Behind my back. [laughs]

A JOYFUL PROCESS

CALVIN: Everyone was singing back then. There was Sammy [Campbell] and the Del Larks and the Bel-Aires. The three of us we used to battle, boy, like at the skating ring and Plainfield High School. Fuzzy was the lead singer of the Bel-Aires, and Raymond was the bass singer of the Del Larks. We used to beat them all the time, and they used to get mad!

FUZZY: With Ray's voice, and Sammy had that crooning thang, the Del Larks were sporty and good like us all. The Bel-Aires—we recorded a few 45s.

GRADY: The Parliaments—out of the three groups, we was the baddest. We used to kick their butts.

FUZZY: Nah, I don't think so. That's why the Parliaments recruited me and Ray, 'cause they needed help. Their guys was quittin'. They couldn't even hold the group together. Anyway, George and I, we started putting shows together. We'd go to Queens Booking Agency and hire a group like the Isley Brothers as a main act, and then hire the local groups like ourselves. We'd be the promoters and the singers.

CALVIN: Everywhere we would go, we were starting to attract a crowd—especially girls—because we weren't bad lookin', could dance, dressed cool, talked cool, and wherever the girls go, the hard heads are gonna follow! We were all like six-feet-something; we were clean and had those processes and those nice pink satin suits and routines; the girls would go crazy. Usually the Bel-Aires would open, then Sammy's group would be next to last, then we'd always close the show. Then when we released that song "Poor Willie," done with ABC/Paramount, we got a lot of local airplay, which put us head and shoulders above the other local groups. The music was R&B, lot of falsetto, pretty harmony, and bass: typical of Frankie Lymon and Teenagers. We started wearing "Parliaments" sweaters.

We sat down one day and decided, hey, we need Fuzzy out of the Bel-Aires, 'cause he was the one who had all the energy, and Raymond out of the Del Larks, 'cause he was the best bass singer around; so we took the best of each to complete our group. We went and kidnapped them. Made them an offer they couldn't refuse!

FUZZY: I joined when I was just coming out of high school, '60, '61. The Bel-Aires had just gotten some bad uniforms—we killed [the Parliaments]. The Parliaments had grey suits and some floppy gold shoes that I inherited from the guy who left the group.

GRADY: I'm the one who fooled [Ray's] butt in there.

(left to right) Calvin Simon, Fuzzy Haskins, and Grady Thomas.

See, I was the bass singer at the time and I was good, but Ray Davis was so ridiculously *bad* with his voice all down in the basement, in the gravel. I told George, "Let me move up to baritone, and let's get Ray Davis!"

FUZZY: No no no, now wait a minute. I'll tell you exactly how we got Ray. We had Larry Fisher at the time, but we wanted to add a bass singer. Your voice was deep, but it was more baritone.

GRADY: That's what I'm saying. I was baritone and bass at the time, but Ray was so doggone bad, so I said to George, "Let's see if we can get Ray, and I'll move to baritone." And Ray was glad to come over to us, 'cause we were still kickin' their butts like—

FUZZY: No no, they weren't doin' nothing. Me and Ray got into the group, *then* you were doin' something. The Bel-Aires was killin' the Parliaments. [*laughs*] Okay, next question!

CALVIN: So I'd sing falsetto, normal, first tenor, and sometimes baritone. Fuzzy'd sing lead, George would sing some lead, Grady baritone, and Ray some lead and bass.

FUZZY: That incident with the money at Plainfield High School, I was playing a little guitar then—only had three strings on it—and I could play the chords to "Gypsy Woman." So I'm sitting on the stool playing the guitar and singing the lead, and then I don't know who told who to throw money, but they began to throw money from the balcony and money was hitting us all in the face: fifty-cent pieces and quarters.

GRADY: George came up with that one. We gave a few people some change to get it started. Then it just caught on. We're up there singing and picking up money at the same time.

CALVIN: We had to do what we had to do. It started a trend. A couple of girls started throwing money up on the stage and, hey, we started picking it up. [It] was an early audience-participation game. We always got the audience involved. That was one of the kind of things that got us ahead. You gotta remember ninety-nine percent of the people coming to see you fantasize about being up on that stage for an hour or two. And you give them something exciting and fun, a lot of clowning around, but with serious harmony and precise routine. We were tight, man. You'd see one, you see us all; we did *everything* together and I do emphasize *everything*! We made a pact, a bond, that we was gonna conquer the world, be as big as the Beatles!

FUZZY: We were becoming young men. We began to gel. We had five guys who had the same goal in mind and never wanted to hang out on the street corners like thugs.

CALVIN: We moved to Plainfield, 'cause they didn't have anyone in the area who was doing hair like us, stuff like the Pin Curl and the Finger Wave. Me, George, and occasionally Grady—'cause he could do hair as well—we kind of made a family business out of it: the Black Soap Palace.

(front row, left to right) Calvin Simon, Ray Davis, and Grady Thomas; (background) Eddie Hazel, Tawl Ross, and Bernie Worrell.

I think [co-owner] Ernie Harris came up with that name. That barbershop—man, everything went on in there. You name it, and we would have to claim it! [*laughs*]

Everyone wanted to hang out there: Billy Nelson, Eddie Hazel, Garry Shider, little snot-nosed kids six to seven years old, man, running around, just wanted to hang out with the big boys. And Bernie [Worrell], he'd sneak out the house and his mother would come and drag him out of there,

'cause she wanted him to practice that piano, not hang out with us! A lot of times after I got really good, George would have to go to Detroit [to shop around the Parliaments' demo tapes], and when he went, I would run the shop, take care of his customers, the business, as he was trying to get contracts for us. So George was always kind of like our front door on the business end of things, but the rest of us held down the other end of the business. And it was cheaper to send one person than to send all of us.

STANDING ON THE VERGE

CALVIN: September 22, 1962—I'll never forget—we went to Motown to audition. Mickey Stevenson is the one who auditioned us. Seven of us (we also had a guitar player Andy Birks at the time) with luggage and guitar got into a 1956 Roadmaster Buick. [*howls with laughter*] We had this driver named Slick who was a mechanic in case something happened. On the way out there on the Pennsylvania Turnpike, the car ran hot. In the middle of the night, out in the middle of nowhere—all you could see was cows and electrical poles. We're in our nice gator shoes, our sharkskin suits, and we had to walk down in the cow pasture, crawlin' with these dome-shaped hubcaps we took off the car. We made a line taking the cows' muddy drinking water, and put it in the car! [*laughs*]

Anyway, we made it to Detroit, all crammed for fourteen hours up on each other slobbering and breaking wind. At the time, Motown only had those three little houses they were working on, and, when we came in, Martha Reeves was the receptionist—she hadn't recorded yet. And as we were going up the steps, Diana Ross and the Supremes were in another room rehearsing this song called "You Doin' Me Wrong." We went and did our interview and smoked it, but, at the time, we looked and sounded so much like the Temptations, Stevenson passed on us, which I can understand.

FUZZY: But then the professional doors began to open for the Parliaments. We was in New York every night hanging out in the Brill building when Jobete opened over there.

GRADY: We had an old little bitty funky office.

FUZZY: Right next to the CBS building, Ed Sullivan's. We were upstairs hanging out the window. All we had was a piano and a desk. I remember seeing Jimi Hendrix sitting in the hallway up there on the floor with his chick and his guitar. Me, George, and Ernie Harris teamed up as writing partners. We was doing a lot of masters for Motown, trying to get someone to take this song, trying to get a deal. George Kerr was a hard taskmaster. I saw him punch someone, the engineer or someone, in the stomach for doing something wrong. Alonzo Tucker—with his cashmere coat on and hat to the side; [he] sounded like Jimmy Durante sometimes—he'd have us by the piano singing, teaching us how to take parts, do whole notes, half notes, top notes. We recorded some 45s.

GRADY: We were listening to the best: the Beatles, Miracles, Temptations, Gladys Knight, Stevie Wonder, lot of gospel groups like the Soul Stirrers.

FUZZY: Then Calvin went off to Vietnam.

CALVIN: I went draggin' and kickin' when they drafted me in '66. I did the math: I only had to go for two years, and if I didn't go, I'd go to jail for five. I was in artillery, loading and breaking up ammo. I left as a sergeant. I was right in the middle of the Tet Offensive. People don't realize how heavy it was back then, man. There were several times I didn't think I'd come back. You're in the jungle—no lights, anaconda snakes, rats, tigers, elephants. Wow. And then you got these fools in black pajamas trying to kill you. All day long, they in your camp doin' your clothes, bringin' ya women in and everything else, and then at night, they put their black pajamas on and mortar you from a hilltop! [laughs] I'm on one hundred percent disability now, 'cause I'm still sufferin'. Once you have to kill people, you never get over that. Plus, when we came home, they gave us a Band-Aid and aspirin and took our M-16s and .45s away. The sad part of it is there's a part of you that wakes up in the morning lookin' to see blood or cause harm; you get addicted to that. They never helped us cope with this. To tell you the truth, if it wasn't for that good ol' herb and stuff in the early days, I don't know what would've happened, 'cause it actually kept me kind of calm. After I came home, I carried a .45 everyday, and being out with all the guys and that craziness, it's just by the grace of God I didn't blow up and hurt somebody, 'cause I couldn't stand to be around crowds after being shot at. Fear, wow, that's a heavy word. After years, I've finally put it in a place where I could deal with it. Fear brought me back across the pond. I sleep soundest sleeping on my back, holding my M-16. And they took it away from me in '68.

FUZZY: Temptations was number one. We tried to be like them with the ties, the shoes, the moves, the routines. But George would always have something missing—always be a little sloppy, missing a tie or shirt or something. We had the hit record with "Testify," number one in New York City, and we had the O'Jays on the show with us at the Apollo Theater, our first real professional gig. The O'Jays were pros, tight, and here we come unschooled, giggling, got the stars' dressing room. The O'Jays—they have to walk up all them stairs. But we bombed. It was the most embarrassing thing that happened to me in the music business.

GRADY: Everyone expected so much from us, and we just blew it. That brought us back down.

FUZZY: How it worked was when one show closed down one week, the next show coming in was supposed to rehearse with the band director, who at the time was Reuben Phillips. You had to get with the [house] band, so they could learn your charts. I did not go to the rehearsal; George, Billy, and Grady went. Billy was in the group playing guitar.

GRADY: We found some old guy to write us some sheet music, and he wrote it like some melancholy music. So we're trying to get the horn lines right with Ruben, 'cause it sounded so doggone crazy.

FUZZY: We start the first show doin' "Testify" and a couple of Motown songs: one was an instrumental ["Six by Six"] to do some dance steps to, and the Four Tops' "7-Rooms of Gloom," [which] starts with one tempo then picks up. I was leading the song, "I see a house…." [but] the music wasn't there, the violins were all over the place, and it was horrible, embarrassing. All I could do was look up in the balcony. [laughs] When the curtain closed, we all run behind the curtains, and Ruben Phillips let out some cursing words.

The younger Funkadelics brought a new fashion sense.

GRADY: So they took our star spot and put the O'Jays on. But each show got better and better.

FUZZY: By the end, we got standing ovations. It was a learning thing. The O'Jays tease us to this day. If you see them, ask 'em if they need the Parliaments to open for them! That was the story line all our career. We called it stoogin' it up, like the Three Stooges. We stooged everything up, everything! Nothing ever ever goes like planned! Our first limousine—remember how excited we were, Grady? We ended up pushing that limousine.

GRADY: Called it a "lemonsine."

FUZZY: We had started touring with "Testify" in '67, then moved to Detroit to the Twenty Grand Motel on the corner of 14th and Warren. [Golden World Records owner] Ed Wingate owned the hotel. That's where we had to dive during the riots. We was on the floor; people getting their fingers, arms, wrists cut off for their jewelry. National Guard had us all pinned up against the wall. Took our uniforms out of the car, stomping on them, lookin' for weapons. We were just afraid of being shot.

GRADY: We renamed it the Shoot 'n' Cut.

CALVIN: "Testify" came out, and I'm being attacked with mortars, and the DJ is on the radio saying, "This goes out to Sgt. Simon. Hope he comes home safely soon." It was surreal. I'd get letters from the guys about who was crashing what cars, 'cause they were touring. When I came

(left to right) Calvin Simon, George Clinton, and Fuzzy Haskins.

home, I took my place back. Before I left, we all had signed a contract with Revilot records. LeBaron [Taylor] had heard "Heart Trouble" from [when we were on] Golden World and so he signed with us. So I met with George and the guys, and there had been quite a transformation within the group: they had goatees, Afros; I didn't recognize them hardly.

FUZZY: We were the Parliaments in suit and tie when Calvin left. But when he came back, let me tell you something. I met Calvin on Plainfield Avenue when he was in his army suit. I had sandals on, a beard, and a straw hat. And I was shaking Calvin's hand—you know Calvin's like 6' 5" and I'm like 5' 5". I wouldn't let his hand go: "Calvin, it's me Fuzzy!" He did not want to be there. And he quit the group, and went back to working for General Motors. He quit the group a few times, couldn't make up his mind. Until he saw all the attention we were getting. Finally, we got him out of that soldier uniform. After we funked him up, we had to funkify him.

GRADY: We had to baptize his butt in the funk again.

LET'S TAKE IT TO THE STAGE

CALVIN: My first thing was to get my money straight. I asked George, "What's goin' on with the money?" He looked at me, smiled, and said, "Ain't no money. LeBaron messed up all the money, man." So I demanded a meeting with all of us at the Twenty Grand Motel in Detroit. All of us showed except George. LeBaron showed up with this big box of cancelled checks. Even Grady, Fuzzy, and Ray didn't know. LeBaron showing us $50,000 here, $70,000 there. They had pockets of money, more than they ever had, but it was only a fraction of what they should've received. George had been taking money. Shortly after that, we formed Parliafunkadelicment Thang Inc. to give everybody a share of both of the [band] names, in writing. Each one of us owned, I think, eleven or thirteen percent and George owned, I think, fifteen or twenty percent, 'cause he was the producer as well.

FUZZY: We had the Parliaments and then Funkadelic. The Parliaments were the five singers and Funkadelic was the band: Billy, Eddie, Tiki, and Tawl. Billy and Eddie, really, was with us right from the beginning.

CALVIN: With Funkadelic, we were the same five singers but instead of being smooth and silky like the Parliaments, we came with the hard acid-rock guitars.

GRADY: I think Billy went and found Eddie Hazel. We had rehearsal up at my house on West 3rd Street, and we ended up telling him, "Don't call us, we'll call you." He just didn't hit us off right away. And then he came back, and he was the tightest thing you have ever seen.

FUZZY: Well, we didn't have nothin' really to hit off on at that time. I think Eddie was commuting back and forth to New York City doing sessions.

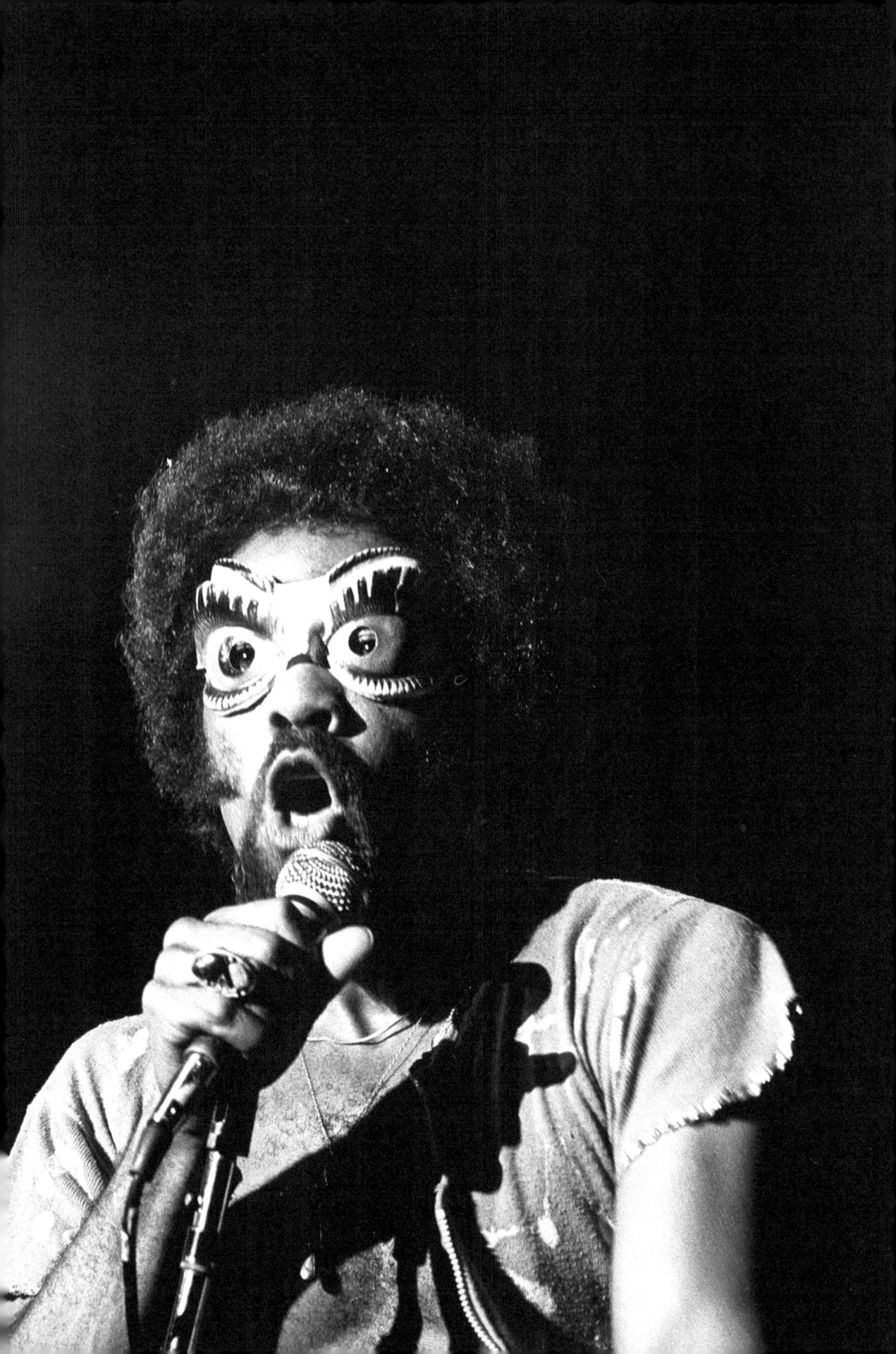

CALVIN: Billy originally started on guitar, then moved to bass, 'cause Eddie was a heck of a guitar player. They were both teenagers. People also don't realize how good Eddie and Billy could sing. But when I came home, I was personally upset, because I felt George had let things get out of hand. I felt that if I had been home, I wouldn't have let Billy and Eddie and the guys get involved in the drugs the way they were. We were supposed to be the older brothers, and through the years, the drug problems really got out of hand. When you're feeling good, you ain't thinking about the business. It's just by the grace of God that I'm here and not in jail or worse.

FUZZY: Billy changed up to that big ol' bass—couldn't even have a case with that thick sucker. That bass was bigger than he was, but he learned how to play, man, and he's one of the better bass players today. Be getting on the planes, bass on his back poppin' old ladies upside the head, goin' down the aisle with his mouth stuck out. "Why don't you move?!" Those guys were one of a kind.

GRADY: Eddie'd pawn his guitar, then borrow someone else's guitar—they loved him so much—and he'd pawn that.

FUZZY: Sometimes, guys would just come and sit in and then just stick around. Like, before we had Tiki [on drums], we had this guy Stacy from D.C. who was a state trooper; he couldn't play that good—I don't know how we got that boy. Tiki was playing at [Philadelphia's] Uptown Theater in the house band. We were out front singing, and, all of a sudden, we hear this rumble, and we said, "Good God, who the heck is this?"

GRADY: He was in from there. The other guy just got up and left.

FUZZY: Tiki'd be out somewhere with Eddie, and I'd have to play drums. Tiki didn't like that. He'd come wearin' that shoulder bag and hat with a cigarette hangin' out his mouth, take the sticks, and show off before he sat down. "I'm here now, I'm the drummer, I'm the bad one," and do a drum roll [for] two minutes with that one stick. Tiki was bad. He didn't have a regular-sized bass drum—his was twenty-six inches, silver.

GRADY: And he'd hit that bass drum so hard, [it'd] knock people up from their seats. Tawl came a little bit later. He was real straight and clean when he got there, and the next thing you know he was off the hook.

FUZZY: [Tawl] had a personality like Iggy Pop. Out there like that. He had people thinking he was insane. But we would exaggerate things on purpose. George would start doin' things too, like look at people and open your eyes real wide like you were nuts. Do anything, do what they don't think that I'll do.

And then when Bernie came in, he was the Krazy Glue that held everything together. Bernie was responsible for all the hits you listening to. His knowledge of music, his keyboard playing, he's a genius. Man, Bernie was doing concerts in a tuxedo when he was four years old! Guys who know music, other serious musicians, know he's a genius. He can play *anything*. Our stuff was loose; we didn't have that musical knowledge. [Bernie's] got perfect pitch. He had this little horn keyboard thing he'd carry around in his back pocket and a car horn would blow and he'd tell you, "B-flat," and then prove it and play it on that melodica.

CALVIN: Bernie grew up with us. And he knew what we were all about, but he had all the technical expertise to go with it. Musically, we wouldn't have made it as far as we did without the expertise of Bernie Worrell. 'Cause Bernie, man, he'd just make the hair on my arms stand up. And he can still do it! He was an anchor for everyone else to freak out. And George never gave Bernie the credit he deserved, because all the musicians would come up with all these lines and stuff, but then after everything was recorded, George would go off by himself and add all these crazy lyrics. He couldn't have done that if the music wasn't already formed.

FUZZY: So we started recording for Westbound around '68.

CALVIN: I still see [Westbound owner] Armen [Boladian]—got his good and bad points. I still have to give him the credit. If it hadn't been for him, Parliament and Funkadelic wouldn't have made it. He took a huge chance. With Funkadelic, it allowed us to have a livelihood until we could resurrect the Parliaments from the dead. No Funkadelic, then there wouldn't have been Parliament. Gotta give credit where it's due. If our names had appeared on those Funkadelic albums, [Revilot owner LeBaron Taylor] would've sued the pants off of us. That's the only reason [Westbound] would let us do Funkadelic, 'cause we had to guarantee [Armen] that we [the Parliaments] would be the singers and would be in control of the situation, but we had to be careful.

The early album covers were cool. [The *Free Your Mind* cover model] was a high-class model from New York City, and here we had her doin' crazy stuff; we kind of freaked her out. And then we had Pedro Bell and those covers, and people thought we were out of our minds, which we were! Pedro Bell made up his own vocabulary.

FUZZY: There were plenty of great songs. We were sleeping in the studio then. We just be doing tracks a lot of time. Always recording. Take some of this, some of that; you didn't know what was gonna be the result. We would trade leads. Then we had *Osmium* with Holland-Dozier-Holland under the Parliaments. You hear me yodeling on "Little Old Country Boy"? And "Good Old Music" was a hit in Detroit. I'm playing drums on "Can You Get to That?"

GRADY: There were a few things that happened that we just started on stage: vocals, a melody thing, then George would slip away to the studio later and we get no kind of writer's [credit]. I was just so enchanted by being out there, I wasn't thinking about any kind of business. I was doin' too much enjoying. "Super Stupid" is about doing drugs. [*he sings*] That's when George was kind of straight and comin' down on them guys with their heroin habits. Cocaine was semi-cool with him.

FUZZY: He was doin' it as he was singing about it. [*laughs*] That coke had you flyin'. I'd feel like I could go joggin' with a Volkswagen on my back. Later on when I read about it, I realized I was playing Russian roulette, man. I thank God today my heart didn't burst.

(*opposite*) Fuzzy Haskins donning his alien mask.

Fuzzy Haskins and the eye of the pyramid.

FREE YOUR MIND AND YOUR ASS WILL FOLLOW

CALVIN: So you get influenced with the drugs and you start listening to Jimi Hendrix and Vanilla Fudge, which were huge at the time. One night we were opening for them, the guys' equipment didn't show up, so Vanilla Fudge let Billy and Eddie use their equipment, which was really unheard of in those days. They started playing and everyone went crazy. We realized how much of an influence you could have with a crowd. But in the infancy of it, we didn't understand all those big amps and all the power, so sometimes it came off as a big blur.

FUZZY: Anything goes—that was our thing. That's when I got into the long johns with the flap in the back; I loved them after they got raggedy in the crotch, strings hangin' down. And the buccaneer boots, the buccaneer hat, beard, and glasses. Controversy brings attention. We blew their minds. We'd do shows with people like the Spinners, and they all thought we were crazy. We exaggerated, played the music louder on purpose. People'd come talking about

hat and everything, with a ring and watch on my bare feet; they called me the Wizard. We wanted to make a statement. It was a mockery, really. You don't only have to have a white sheet on, you got Klan people who don't have any sheets on at all. I used to paint my face going back to African relatives; there was significance to it.

GRADY: I started being a sheik. That Arab shit thing. I just didn't have my harem (well, I did but…).

FUZZY: See, Queens [Booking] was sending out those pictures of the five of us in those suits and processed hair. Then when clubs hired us and we got to the venue, they said, "Oh my God, what the heck are these guys doin'?" Then George started doing this acting stuff. Laying out on tables, on people's drinks, and crawling on the floor naked with just a sheet on and with that Mohawk haircut.

GRADY: And that's what got people coming to the shows; they couldn't believe what people were saying. It was spectacular. We were crazy, wild, and playing good, hard, funky music. And people would come in as skeptical as the devil, comin' in all cool, straight, all cute, and, boy, next thing, we comin' intense from beginning to end. Some of them would back way out, [but] after we got a hold of them, they just couldn't stop jamming.

CALVIN: Show would start with the band crankin', feedback, then as they started a groove, we would come out in a line: George, Fuzzy, then me, then Grady, then Raymond.

FUZZY: I had this little saying, funk is F-U-N with a special K, and the K was the kids we wanted to come and have fun with us, come out of the misery some of 'em were in, and spend two to three hours a night at [our] concert. And that's how we started out. Funkadelic was fun. Not stinkin' and sweatin', not that funk, but having fun with a special K—the K representing every kid in America that loved our music.

CALVIN: We took it to another level. Most of our crowd at that time was those college kids—mostly White rock crowds. We'd open up for Ted Nugent, MC5, Chicago, Leon Russell, Blood, Sweat and Tears, just about everybody. They were good, but when we finished, the audience was exhausted. We were such high energy, they didn't want to hear nothing else after that. *Everyone* wanted to get in and get out before we started, 'cause it was on!

FUZZY: George, he'd put a hole in the middle of the sheet, put lipstick on it, then walk downtown. Remember in Toronto, we was downtown, and George farted on that little White kid? Me, Grady, and George are walking down Young Street. This little kid was shining shoes, and he ran up behind George and yelled, "What you got on under there?" and pulled his sheet up. And George let one go on his head. "Hey, you nasty pig!" the kid yelled. [*laughter*] And then of course there was the time we got locked up while tripping on acid. We were playing the Hawk's Nest, and we ran out on the hotel bill. We were so far gone and crazy-lookin', even the drunks in jail were freaked out.

CALVIN: We were at the frontier, man. Everything was new then. At first, a lot of people thought they were derogatory terms. "Free Your Mind and Your Ass Will Follow"—when you first think about it is like *what*, what did he just say? [*laughs*] But all we were saying was if you get your head

the Temptations, but after we finished with them they had something to run and tell. The publicity we were getting was: "Those guys'll bust your eardrums!" They weren't talking about no Temptations. We had found our identity. Sly Stone got a hit record before us, but we changed the world for entertainment as far as for these suits and ties.

CALVIN: We would scare people sometimes because we were so wild, raw, and crazy. I've seen girls flat out running away in their stockings trying to get away from us! You gotta remember, man, I had on a blue Klan robe with the

WAXPOETICS 53

together, the rest of you will come along. If you get your books and your education, then the rest of your body will *have* to come along. Then we got exposed to the bigger acts; we started to define our sound. To me, it was more interesting in the early days, 'cause we were making statements: "Super Stupid," "Maggot Brain," "Cosmic Slop": those songs had meaning. Then it mostly became about the party, depending on what you were doing that night and where your head was. And free love was in effect the whole time.

FUZZY: We was movin' up, getting exposure that a lot of Black groups weren't getting at that time. We've gone places and people thought we were White, and we'd get there and there was a fit. Happened at the Sugar Shack in Boston. Rudy [the owner] thought we were White because of our sound, but then Rudy saw the pictures of the five of us, and we didn't even match the pictures! Thirteen of us dressed the way we were dressed, he said, "No way are you comin' up in here looking like that!"

GRADY: "Get out of here. You're not the Parliaments!" But after one show, he was down 'cause we turned them out. All the pimps and prostitutes—they was in there all skeptical. I could *feel* it coming from everybody. We come out all crazy, jumping on tables, and then, boy, they just loved it. The Sugar Shack at that time used to have a lot of pimps and hoes in there, and, man, the pimps, they was hating us at first, 'cause all their prostitutes was coming down to the show instead of working, and they was all peeved at them, beating them up and stuff. They'd come down to the show to get their girls, then before you know it, they'd try to be all friendly, bringin' us drugs and whatever we wanted.

FUZZY: That was the main thing then, we were getting our fill of *everything*. That's what the funk was about: a joint rolled in toilet paper.

GRADY: Acid.

FUZZY: We went to London and they all came out, 'cause they heard about all the stuff we did with the donkey at Royal Albert Hall. Just for publicity, we had a donkey up on the steps of RAH, you know, to say, "Hey, look for these crazy Funkadelics in town." And the donkey took a crap all over the steps! I don't know where they got him from, [must've] got him from the donkey farm. Look look, they heard that we were funky, right? So they got a donkey; they got it mixed up.

GRADY: We really wasn't that popular over there. We were gonna try to play RAH and they wouldn't let us play there, so that's when we got a donkey. That just got all around Europe, and all the rest of the places we played was packin'. Led Zeppelin and Pete Townsend came by and checked us out.

CALVIN: We were touring England [in 1971], and everyone came to check us out. I think it was the Underground Railroad or something, and guess who was sitting next to Bernie? Was almost his roadie for two weeks: Herbie Hancock. Man, he was so into Bernie, if Bernie had made a quick move, he would've broke Herbie Hancock's neck.

THE UP BEFORE THE DOWN STROKE

CALVIN: Soon we were filling up arenas, then stadiums—the first Black group to do it. We toured with Mandrill for a couple of years. They had more fun with us than they had with anybody else! Them and Osibisa. Loved them. We didn't have any beefs. Only time we had a problem was one time we did a show with War, they came out after us and the stage was so hot, we'd torn it up and left the people in such a frenzy, that the lead singer of War came out and told the audience, "Okay, now let's do some real music." Oh, he shouldn't've said that. [*laughs*] They were kind of like a mellow-type group, so people were leaving their show in droves.

GRADY: The Temp—I mean—Imitations, they stole some of our music.

FUZZY: That was Norman Whitfield. "Psychedelic Shack"—they took that from our show. They wasn't tryin' to hide it. Norman brought his tape recorder and set it up on this table right in front of the stage. He just used the guitar part. Everybody knew he did. We didn't really care.

Then Eddie, Billy, Tiki jumped ship. But George always come up with some idea. We got Bootsy's group in the woods in a cabin in Canada. I think Bootsy stayed with us about two years and played as Funkadelic. Didn't no one know, wasn't no Bootsy band, it was Parliament-Funkadelic. It made everything better.

GRADY: That's when we got playing more horns. Got Maceo and Fred—the best.

CALVIN: Then when we came out with that Mothership, man. With George Fisher designing our stage, we were right up there with Elton John [and] the Rolling Stones! To this day, people still don't understand the significance of having that Mothership Connection. They don't realize the history behind all that and what we had to do to put that on, and what the record company had to do. Neil Bogart, man, he was something else; he didn't mind spending the money. We had over a hundred people in our crew. Between [Casablanca] and Warner Brothers, it cost about a million and a half dollars to put that whole Mothership production together, and, remember, at that time, a million and a half dollars was a million and a half dollars. One of my biggest beefs with George was we could've taken that whole show to Broadway, 'cause there was nothing like that ever. It could've been the first funk opera to hit Broadway. But George wasn't disciplined enough to do it.

A WHOLE LOT OF B.S.

FUZZY: I never thought I'd have a feeling of not wanting to be on that stage. It came when me and Grady were singing behind that amplifier [on Mothership tour]. That was so funny.

GRADY: No it wasn't… You're married and gotta come home and [answer], "How come George's wife got all this?" And you know, lot of people thought we was getting money and just throwin' it.

FUZZY: Not at the time, but now it's funny. Didn't think things would ever go that way. Here we are, we've been friends forever, all five of us. Didn't think that would happen. In conversation, George would always say "we we we," but it wasn't really that way. When George was putting the Mothership

Tour together, that's when a thick portion of it happened. He hired backstage management, a personal manager. Hold up five fingers and put eight more fingers between the thumb and those other fingers. The four fingers over here are me, Calvin, Grady, and Ray. Between the thumb and the fingers are all the other people. And you had to go through them to get to George. Then they started to stay at other hotels. It just grew out of that. Pacify you with travel, take a girl home, and get high. Never take no money home.

All of our families were having problems, 'cause they wanted to see the money. Here we are in all these magazines, *Jet, Ebony*, people talking about how we got the top record in the land. At first, we had our pockets stuffed. But George weeded it out, worked it away, worked it around. Just signed himself to the companies, and got the companies to buy into that. Westbound, Casablanca…

CALVIN: The bigger the headache, the bigger the pill, as they say.

FUZZY: We never had a manager per se. It came with the money and greed, then the takeover—the hostile takeover. George's idea was, since we all lived now close to New York City, we should move the company to New York. This was '76. Idea started in '75. I remember 'cause I did a solo record with Westbound in '76, 'cause I saw the writing on the wall. So the summer part of '76, after my album came out, George comes forth with the papers to sign for the new company called Thang, Inc. and that George owned it himself. If you signed it, then you'd be an employee of Thang, Inc., of which we should be shared owners of, if anything. So he offered everybody cars if they signed and a few dollars. Grady and I were the only ones not to sign. It could've been a million dollars, we weren't goin' for that. It was just crazy. He bought everyone out with a leased car and a few dollars. That's what it was, and you can print that!

GRADY: I ain't no lawyer and nowhere near one, but that contract stood out telling us if you sign here you lose the rights to Parliament-Funkadelic. I was enraged.

FUZZY: We did the music for *One Nation* [then left]. But here's the kicker. He had Cecil Holmes from Casablanca go to Washington and they took the "s" out of Parliaments, so you know what that meant. That "s" represented the four of us, and [they] plucked it right off. [*laughs*] Man, that's a good one!

See, and people wonder what happened, they want to know the truth, they come and ask us. And I've seen interviews with George and he'll say, "Well, I wanted a spaceship, all of them wanted cars." That's the most ridiculous thing. Sure maybe everybody wanted a car, but not under those circumstances. The guy asked George, "Are they getting paid?" and George says, "They're still here, aren't they?" [*laughs*] But hey, that's how it went, man. I think back to how we [used to] rehearse out there in Potter's Crossing in a little shed, night after night, singing and rehearsing, just to maybe get a chance to start in the music business, get a hit record. You want to get your families out of the ghetto, buy a house for your mom, take care of your children, and that's every musician's dream.

I don't think we even realized how people felt about us and what we had, 'cause I don't believe maybe George would've done what he wound up doin'. I don't think he wanted it to be like this, to end up this way. We had something very unique. It was a shame, because we're playing all this great music and having fun, but when it came time to divvy up the money, it seemed the money was never ever there.

But I can say this, we are more happy now with our own group, Original P. We've made a name for ourselves; we're in the mix. All the true deep-hearted funkateers know. I feel we were betrayed, but I feel we betrayed a lot of people too, 'cause they didn't know what really happened. They knew something happened but didn't know what exactly.

CALVIN: Before the Garrys, the Billy Nelsons, Eddies, Bernies, Junies, it was George, Fuzzy, Grady, Calvin, and Ray. And for years, our families suffered, man, for what we were trying to do. I spent a lot of my personal money keeping this group together, tore up a lot of my cars running up and down the roads with this group. That's what really gets me—is the sacrifices we made, and *to this day* have not been repaid. And the good thing, thank God, I never just relied on the group; otherwise, I wouldn't be a millionaire today. Parliament-Funkadelic has never done anything for me, financially. But it's the fact of what George did to us, the bond that he broke with the deceit and the greed, man, that was the most hurtful. To the point where I even contemplated taking George out, period. And by just getting back from Vietnam, it wouldn't've taken much for me to do that.

George did a lot of things to a lot of people that the public just don't know about. And he's such a lovable guy, man, he could sell ice to an Eskimo. George couldn't have did it by himself, but by him standing on our shoulders and pulling this thing off, and then once it's pulled off, we standing there waiting for our reward, we get kicked in the teeth. That's like walking into a back-end mule kick! [*laughs*] You expect to be attacked from the world but not to be attacked from the inside out, and when you go inside and take the heart out, that's a tough thing. A real tough thing. And with George, even today, we don't talk. I left the group in '78 and haven't been back to this day. I didn't even deal with the group till we got inducted into the Rock and Roll Hall of Fame in '97.

G. C., he's a mastermind, I give him credit. But I know, and George knows I know, the real story. He doesn't want the real story told till after he's dead and gone. There's so much that some stuff will probably never be told and probably shouldn't be. I enjoyed talking with you. I know I'm gonna be messed up for a couple of days, having conjured up all these memories, so I gotta do some praying here. [*laughs*]

FUZZY: I hate to have so much negative stuff on George, 'cause I'm out of that. I still love the guy in some deep, crazy, silly way even after all what's been done to us. He's in my prayers every night—all these guys are, and I start off with his name first. I have nothing harbored up against him. He's made a name for himself—White, Black, so many [people] know George Clinton. A lot of good and negative things have happened along the way, and even he can be straightened out. Everybody's got a shot. I wish him the best. ⊙

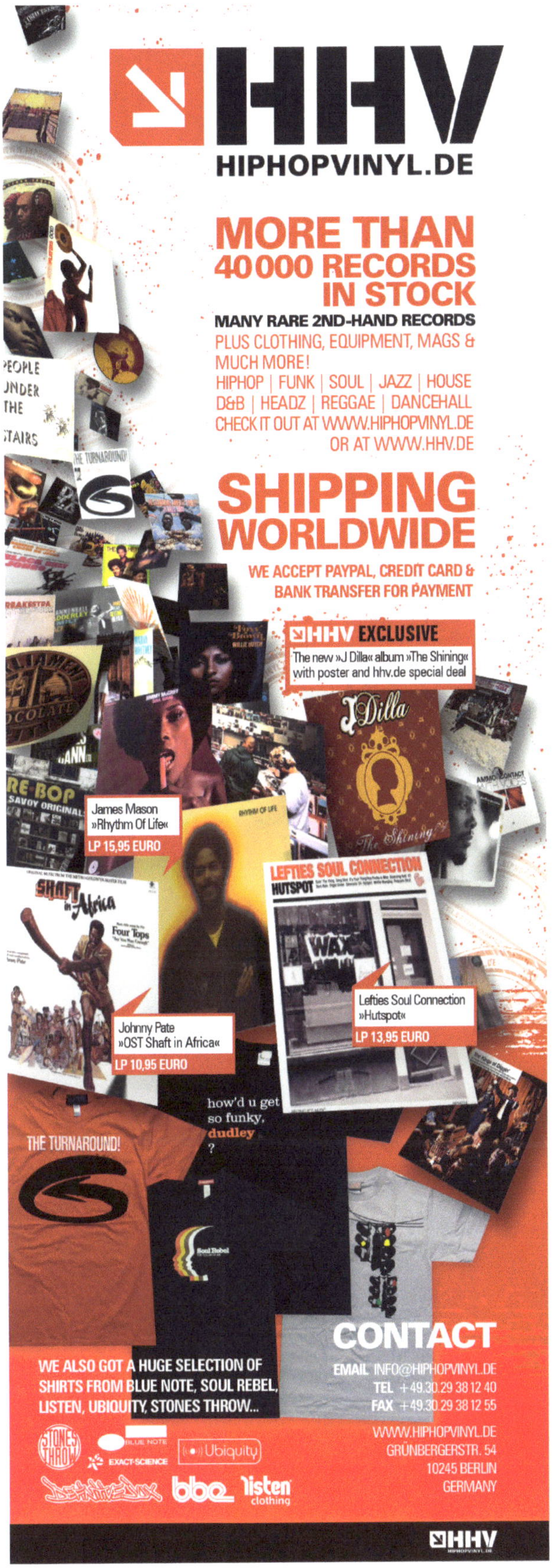

HHV
HIPHOPVINYL.DE

MORE THAN 40 000 RECORDS IN STOCK

MANY RARE 2ND-HAND RECORDS PLUS CLOTHING, EQUIPMENT, MAGS & MUCH MORE!

HIPHOP | FUNK | SOUL | JAZZ | HOUSE
D&B | HEADZ | REGGAE | DANCEHALL
CHECK IT OUT AT WWW.HIPHOPVINYL.DE
OR AT WWW.HHV.DE

SHIPPING WORLDWIDE

WE ACCEPT PAYPAL, CREDIT CARD & BANK TRANSFER FOR PAYMENT

HHV EXCLUSIVE
The new »J Dilla« album »The Shining« with poster and hhv.de special deal

James Mason »Rhythm Of Life«
LP 15,95 EURO

Johnny Pate »OST Shaft in Africa«
LP 10,95 EURO

Lefties Soul Connection »Hutspot«
LP 13,95 EURO

WE ALSO GOT A HUGE SELECTION OF SHIRTS FROM BLUE NOTE, SOUL REBEL, LISTEN, UBIQUITY, STONES THROW...

CONTACT
EMAIL INFO@HIPHOPVINYL.DE
TEL +49.30.29 38 12 40
FAX +49.30.29 38 12 55

WWW.HIPHOPVINYL.DE
GRÜNBERGERSTR. 54
10245 BERLIN
GERMANY

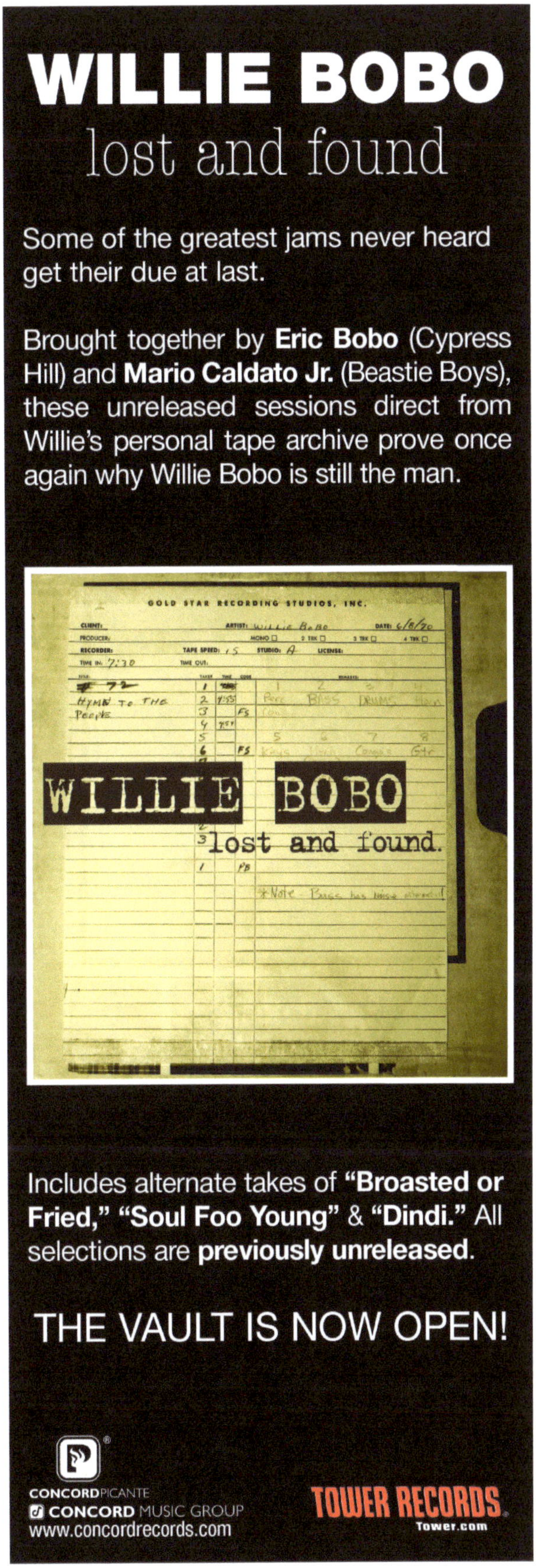

WILLIE BOBO
lost and found

Some of the greatest jams never heard get their due at last.

Brought together by **Eric Bobo** (Cypress Hill) and **Mario Caldato Jr.** (Beastie Boys), these unreleased sessions direct from Willie's personal tape archive prove once again why Willie Bobo is still the man.

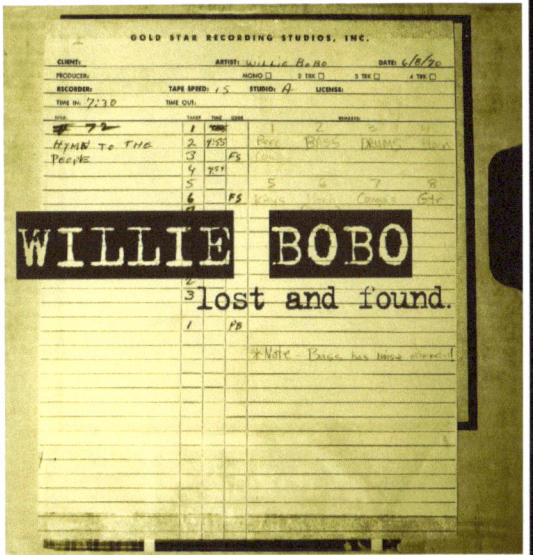

Includes alternate takes of **"Broasted or Fried,"** **"Soul Foo Young"** & **"Dindi."** All selections are **previously unreleased**.

THE VAULT IS NOW OPEN!

CONCORD PICANTE
CONCORD MUSIC GROUP
www.concordrecords.com

TOWER RECORDS
Tower.com

Funkadelic at Cobo Hall, Detroit: (front) Billy "Bass" Nelson; (middle row, left to right) Tiki Fulwood (with snare drum), Eddie Hazel, George Clinton; (back row, left to right) Ray Davis, Calvin Simon, Grady Thomas, Fuzzy Haskins, Tawl Ross, and Bernie Worrell.

MOMMY, WHAT'S A FUNKADELIC?

ORIGINAL PLAYER BILLY "BASS" NELSON GETS TO THE BOTTOM OF IT

by Matt Rogers • photos © Michael Ochs Archives.com

"I was born with a guitar: I believe I was playing my mother's umbilical cord in the womb, 'cause when I came out she says I had the umbilical wrapped around my neck, so they had to put my ass in the incubator. *And* I had a hernia. So I was doin' something in there that I had no business doin'!"

The whole story of Funkadelic is the greatest story never told. ¶ We shocked the whole industry. Everybody wanted to be a Funkadelic by 1969: the Temptations, everybody. We were Detroit's favorite group. To this day, if I'm doing an interview and I say I'm not from Detroit, someone from Detroit is gonna check me. ¶ You're gonna sense some bitterness and I admit it: I'm disappointed, hurt—all that negative bullshit. From time to time it has to come out, 'cause I've been holding a lot of shit in for years. I'm telling it like it is; I don't want to even lie about it. I wish people wouldn't judge me—'cause I'm telling the truth, rather than just bad-mouthing somebody. You think that at the height of our career, I wanted to walk away from Funkadelic? I knew who the fuck we were and what was goin' on. I knew the records were history-making records. I could see everyone in this country wantin' to be like us real soon! The group wasn't even a whole year old before people wanted to dress like us, sound like us. When the radio stations were reluctant to play our material, I knew that *that* was something right there.

People wanna come at me, "You're hostile, you're bitter, you shouldn't be like that." I'm not like that, I'm just telling you what I've experienced, what I've seen: the hand that George Clinton deals to everybody. I've always been the advocate for: "Let's unite and stand up"—the whole industry is fucked up. And it's a shame, man, all that we could have had together. Now you can't take it away from him: George is one of the cleverest songwriters there is, but he didn't get it alone. The reason why he can still work like he still [does] is because of the foundation we laid as the original Funkadelics. The Parliaments didn't play no music.

We represented everything that was new to the music scene—our approach, everything. Nobody that came out during that time was more creative, innovative, or original. We had it. But people were scared of us, the way we looked, and the live performance, man. I've seen audiences part like the Red Sea. When George go running off the stage into the audience, man, people were scared to touch him. People, literally, used to get sick; throwin' up, man, and shit like that.

ME AND MY FOLKS

Plainfield was ideal for growing up; I just stayed in all kinds of trouble. I lived in the projects and used to scrap a lot. If I didn't get my ass whipped before the day was over, I thought something was wrong. I was real tiny then and didn't like being called "short" names. They used to call me midget, runt, half-pint, and I just started fighting.

My dad played guitar in a gospel group called the Stewart Brothers. Me and my pops was tight. He was a major influence musically, [his family] all sang gospel. My grandmother was a mother in the Refuge Church of Christ. Holy sanctified. It's a little different than Baptist. I would say more spiritual. I loved that church.

WAXPOETICS 59

Michael Hampton taking a solo.

Tawl Ross in a famous pose.

There were a lot of serious jazz musicians in Plainfield. There was one blind guy that ran the local cleaners named Jerry. Man, that's who inspired me to play trumpet, 'cause that cat could play. I was in the drum and bugle corps when I was like seven years old. I was first trumpet in the school band—wanted to be Miles Davis, Lee Morgan, Quincy Jones (that "Killer Joe" shit). I was blowing the sax line of "Shotgun," but my dad called it noise. He gave me an acoustic guitar: "You wanna play, play this." I was real bent out of shape about it. First, I learned how to play like my dad, then, [when] I was about ten and a half, I met Eddie Hazel. *That* was beautiful.

It was summertime and everyone was trying to have their band; everybody wanted to be a Motown star. They used to have these jam sessions in people's backyards. I just happened to be walking down the street and could hear this music coming from this guy's backyard. I just thought somebody was playing a record at a party; I eased on back and there was about three guitar players, a bass player, and drummer, and they was getting off! Eddie was one of the guitar players, and you could tell it was Eddie playing the hell out of this song "Wipeout"—sounded just like the record.

I walked up and introduced myself. Before that I still wasn't interested in playing guitar, didn't want to be like my dad. He was eleven, a year older than me. We made a deal: you teach me how to play guitar, and I'll teach you everything I know about singing. I hate to say it, but Eddie was a momma's boy. She didn't allow him too far from the house. He wasn't coming into the projects. His grandmother taught him how to play. We used to call her Ma Bee [Bessie]. She smoked a cigar and played all that gutbucket blues. She was a funky old lady, man—never seen nothing like it, smoking that cigar, drinking some booze, singing, and playing the hell out of that guitar; playing slide with dimes, soda tops, back of a butter knife, anything. Eddie could do all that shit. You listen to "Qualify and Satisfy"—that's where that's coming from. That was Eddie.

BLACK SOAP PALACE

All hell used to break loose in that barbershop; [it] was across the street from the projects. And that's when I met George—in 1958, May 30. I had been hanging out singing and dancing to the jukebox, running errands for people, sweeping up the floor to make my little hustle change. No one's mom wanted their kids there, especially that one. They were selling drugs and everything. All the nasty hoes and shit be hanging out. My uncle whooped my ass in front of everybody and you would've thought that would've been enough to keep me out of there. *Sheeiit*, right back in there the very next day. I was there when Bernie [Worrell] got a head full of sores, 'cause his mother came in there and started beating his ass out of the chair and cursing George and Ernie. I mean, you never heard her curse. Bernie had real thin hair, had no business getting no process; the lye, the chemicals burnt up his hair so bad, his hair started fall-

The Funkadelics: (left to right) Eddie Hazel, Billy Bass (with cap pulled down), Bernie Worrell, Tiki Fulwood, and Tawl Ross.

ing out. [*laughs*] Bernie used to play organ for my mother's gospel chorus and I used to go and sit on the bench while he was playing and watch his fingers. He couldn't have been no more than ten.

Ernie Harris and George [Clinton] were partners. [They] bought the shop off of George White. Now, Ernie, man, that cat was extremely smart—could've been a professor, a scientist, but he was a barber. He had record deals with Duke—this is 1960. The hit on Duke was called "If I" and [there was] a double hit with "Hold On" and "Betty" on Okeh records. Big orchestrated records of the day. Not no funk stuff. Ernie could've been a big star. He was a single artist and he had production—sounded like Brooke Benton. They were preppin' Ernie to be a pop star like Sam Cooke. And he had it. I was just listening to one of those songs, and he's burning a *hole* in Little Anthony's ass. He could sing like fucking Caruso. Draw all his air into his diaphragm—he'd teach me this—then start singing opera like a fucking tenor, and if you're standing next to him you had to get away, 'cause he'd break your eardrum. Ernie taught all of us everything we know, taught George how to really be a fucking entertainer. Ernie wrote many of those lyrics[1], and that's why he died unhappy as far as that situation is concerned. He wasn't mad at George. Before he died, he explained, "I'm not mad at him, but I am disappointed. 'Cause he could've done better."

From when I was eleven to fifteen, I'd go to his house and his wife would cook dinner, and I would try to write songs and he'd teach me—lay stuff down on his tape recorder. He had an electric, I had an acoustic. I would tune the electric like a bass and do double tracks and sing these little corny songs I was writing, and he would write a couple of songs for me. When I was thirteen, Ernie had a deal for me with Columbia Records: he and George had decided they wanted to produce me. But my mother would not let me do it, 'cause they did not want me hangin' in the barbershop.

She said, "If you want to sing so much, you gonna sing in the church." I was just getting more rebellious, 'cause I wanted that record deal. First, she made me get baptized, then made me join the Plainfield Male Chorus. First, she made me and my brother go up there and sing a solo at the pastor's anniversary out of the blue sky, made us learn "How Great Thou Art" by Mahalia Jackson, and, after having been around Ernie, that blew them away. [We] traveled all around New Jersey and as far as Baltimore. And you know what? I got to like it.

I WANNA TESTIFY

It was mainly the Parliaments, the Bel-Aires, Del Larks, and the Wonders. Each group had their own uniqueness, but all wanted to be the Four Tops, Temps—even the instrumental groups. Sammy Campbell—we're cousins—was an inspiration. I played with Sammy and the Wonders for a while before the Parliaments. I had a little band called the Entertainers. Here you got a young Black band playing "I Wanna

The Funkadelics: (front, left to right) Eddie Hazel and Billy Bass; (back, left to right) Tiki Fulwood, Tawl Ross, and Bernie Worrell.

Hold Your Hand"; we used to wear "Satisfaction" out, man.

George was bringing back a lot of Motown stuff from Detroit every weekend—records that wouldn't come out for months. We had Edwin Starr's "Double O Soul" on the jukebox three months before it came out! I was in the barbershop with my guitar playing to the jukebox even when I wasn't working, 'cause they had given me a job by then, cleaning up and helping when people were getting their hair done. And when the [Parliaments] rehearsed, I'd play the guitar along with them. So [after the Boyce brothers][2] went to Vietnam, they said, "You got [the gig]."

Me, George, and Ernie made a demo for "Testify." We started out early in the day at the barbershop, and when it closed, we went to Ernie's house and put it on tape. I played the electric guitar, made it sound like a bass, then tuned it back up to make it sound like a regular guitar. I forget what we used for backbeat, but it wasn't no drums. That weekend, George went to Detroit with that. Me and Ernie definitely should've gotten credit for that song.

[After Revilot released "(I Wanna) Testify"], we heard it on the R&B stations for a week or two. Then, like a bat out of hell, it was on WABC—you know, Cousin Brucie's show. "Testify" was a *pop* record. WABC was *the* top station in this country—in the world—only other station as big would have been the BBC or Radio Luxembourg. We was trippin' big time. 'Cause "Testify" was in the top ten on WABC that

week, we automatically come in as the star of the Apollo show, over the fuckin' O'Jays, the Spinners, the Dominoes, Jo Harris and the Peps, the Vibrations, all these cats that were seasoned veterans, and here we are: stars of the show!

I didn't have my own guitar, so the guitar player from the Peps let me use his. I got nervous, had all these arrangements, and we started doin' "7-Rooms of Gloom" and the [house] band started fuckin' up. I'm not a band director, so I didn't know how to stop and get them on track. Man, the people were throwing shit on the stage and all of that. It was so fucking embarrassing, I cried. After that show, I didn't come back. Plus, the union guy came and I didn't have a union card, so I had to go all the way to Washington DC and get a card. Man, I seen all them groups laughing at them. The only thing is that they had the balls to just go ahead on. I don't think the [Parliaments] starred the rest of the week; they got demoted. That was one of those situations you don't recover from. That's like getting shot between the fucking eyes.

From May to August, we were out there working all over the place: did a lot of theaters like the Uptown, the Howard, with the Spinners, and then were in the clubs with the Four Seasons, Pete Seeger, Mitch Ryder and Detroit Wheels. I finally got a brand new Fender Jaguar—man, great guitar. One night we was in Michigan with the Amboy Dukes, and when Ted Nugent got finished burnin', I was *done*, 'cause I knew I wasn't playin' no guitar like that. To top it off, he took me in the dressing room and show[ed] me some hellacious power chords. After that show, I threw that guitar out the fucking window.

See, I was the only musician in the [group], so we were using house bands the whole time. Gene Page, who was a big arranger in those days, arranged the whole [touring] show around my guitar playing. He showed me some shortcuts, but I was no band director; I didn't know how to cut those motherfuckers off. When it got to the end of the show, the band just kept right on goin'. [*laughs*] I was like, "Fuck this. I know that Eddie'll be able to handle this shit." I hadn't played bass yet, but I knew enough about guitar and had played with Eddie enough emulating the bass line while he was playing lead and singing. When we got to the end of that tour, the whole time we was off, I searched and searched for that muthafucka. His mom didn't want to tell me where he was, but I found out he was actually at George Blackwell's[3] house. I told him this is the chance we've been waiting for. He was like, "Nah man, fuck them." I begged, "Just go to George's house and talk to him." I don't know what George promised him, but he was down.

My saving grace, thank God, was [that] I had talked with James Jamerson back when we did some sessions in Detroit [for what] was supposed to be the Parliaments first album that never got released. I was playing rhythm guitar and was surrounded by the whole Motown rhythm section: Don Davis, Robert White, Uriel and Pistol, the drummers, Earl Van Dyke. Jamerson let me play his bass, said, "When you switch to bass come and see me." I had told him about Eddie and what I was thinking about. He took me under his wing, told me, "Don't let me catch you doin' nothing wrong now, 'cause I will get into your behind," 'cause I was only sixteen. Anyway, after I got Eddie involved, I hooked up with [Jamerson] a few times. There were four of us goin' to Jamerson and learning—could maybe [be] called his disciples—Michael Henderson was one of them. To [Jamerson's] amazement, I had already been playing his lines. "You got something unique," [he told me.] "You're inventing, finding pockets that wasn't even there. Just concentrate on developing your own style and get a serious bass. Get you a Fender."[4]

We started the tour again and got to the Uptown, and when Tiki heard Eddie and me play, he was like, "Damn, I can get with y'all. Y'all need me." Tiki was with the house band, stealing the show off of the singers. Everyone called him Butch. Stacy, the drummer we had, was not in the ballpark. We kept telling George, [but he'd say,] "Oh man, we already got a drummer. Stacy's good enough." I said, "Man, we gotta figure something out." Tiki was *the* drummer for us. Grady, Fuzzy, and them heard him play with us, but they were so determined that we didn't know what we were talking about. So I hatched the takeover plan. [I told Tiki,] "You gonna have to Bogart. I'm the leader of the band; I say you." So we started the show, got maybe thirty-two bars into one of them cover songs, man, when Tiki started playing. It was so noticeable that Stacy looked behind him, saw Tiki was playing, and just started packing the drums up. And Tiki played the whole show like he'd been playing with us the whole time. It was fucking awesome. Tiki was consistent like that every night. I know that's the way I developed my consistency, 'cause I couldn't be slacking playing with a drummer like him and a guitar player like Eddie. They were both creative and consistent. And brand new.

THIS IS A FUNKADELIC

The Funkadelic name happened when we were out on the road in '67. They wanted us to be known as the Parliaments' *backup* band, and I said no fucking way. "You don't want us to be Parliaments? Guess what, we'll come up with our own name, 'cause we're contributing just as much, and Eddie and I can sing circles around all y'all." We had a Buick station wagon with a trailer hitched on it, and the car was full with the band—all the fucking *shit* that used to go on in that car! On the way to a gig, we were talking about some names, Dells, Del-Vikings, and how everything was "psychedelic" this and "funky" that. Eddie said something stupid like, "We ought to come up with a group called the Del-Funkies"; then it just slipped out my mouth: "What about Funkadelic?" Man, it got real quiet. "Well...there it is," [I said]. "Funkadelic is the name. And you didn't think of it."

Once the Funkadelics were born, we tried the uniform thing but nobody wanted to dress like that! We cut off the processes (I was a Muslim at the time); I started growing my Afro (Eddie already had one)—couldn't grow a mustache but got a little chin fuzz. My favorite designer was Peter Blake (Beatles' *Yellow Submarine*, *Sgt. Pepper's*), so we dressed mod. Cream, Blue Cheer, *Sgt. Pepper's*, Sly, Vanilla Fudge: that's what we were listening to constantly. And once Eddie started listening to Jimi Hendrix, he found his niche. Immediately, he was like, "Damn, Bill, I can do that! Can you play that bass shit, muthafucka?" I was like, "Hey man, I guess I'm gonna have to." For me, it was all about James Jamerson. If you could do that, then anything would be easy.

Well, one night we were playing at Holy Cross opening for Vanilla Fudge, and there was an accident with our equipment truck. Vanilla Fudge said to go ahead, plug into their equipment. The bass player had a double set of Ampeg SVTs—four cabinets and two tops—and a Crown preamp; it was huge, much larger than what I had ever played. The sound was almost unmanageable, and it would've been if I'd been scared. The guitarist had a double stack of Marshalls,

and the drummer had a big ol' set of transparent Fibes[5]. So we all experienced some *serious* equipment that night. And that sound, we realized, was the sound we had been reaching for. All we needed was the amps. And we got 'em.

At that particular point, the Parliaments was under litigation. They couldn't sign contracts with any label, so it was on us. With Westbound, George signed as a producer; we signed as the artist, Funkadelic. It was strictly us, I made sure of that. Later on, we did a thing with Holland-Dozier-Holland, and it was a combination of both groups.[6]

We were so young and wanted to be out there, so contractually we got fucked with the fine print. There is no way every last one of us should not be at least extremely wealthy. But George and the Parliaments saw to it that that wouldn't happen.

SPLITSVILLE AND BACK

We split up the first time the last part of '68. The handwriting was on the wall that fucking soon. The first Funkadelic album hadn't been finished yet. We left and were working on our own with Sparky[7] in Newark as Funkadelic, then as Sparky and the Pimpadelics, [but then] Eddie chickened out and went back to Detroit. In December, I hooked up with Bill Doggett, played with him a few months. One of the most beautiful gigs I ever had playing bass. He was teaching me how to read chord charts, then there were tunes like "Honky Tonk." He'd show me the bass line on the organ, and it was just fucking *unbelievable* when that song came together. That's when I really started seeing there was a magic to music when it all came together—it was just fucking scary. I didn't experience that kind of magic with the music of Funkadelic till I experienced that with Bill Doggett, on the real tip. How, like Jamerson told me, "When you find a pocket, stay—keep it solid." I picked up on all of that when I was with Bill. That was my partner; I loved him.

Well, George knew I was playing with Bill, so he sent word out [that] he wanted me back, and Tiki said only way he was goin' back is if I go. George came to a club in Buffalo I was at, had something "important" to talk about, said we can't finish the album without you, that Eddie's tried to put bands together, but it just ain't working. "We need you and Tiki." So, stupid me gave Bill notice.

Tawl's not been dealing with a full deck since the beginning. I don't remember not knowing Tawl Ross. My mother has pictures of me, Tawl, and my brother in our diapers. We all used to get guitar lessons from Tawl. While I was with Bill, Eddie got Tawl to play bass, got him out of Plainfield. They were playing straight-up R&B—just wasn't working. George told me he wanted me to be leader of the band again. So I immediately called Tiki, who was playing with Tyrone Davis. He got on the next thing smoking out of Chicago. And I started contacting Bernie [Worrell]. We had another keyboard player, Mickey Atkins, that Eddie had found, but his heart wasn't in it.

Bernie would listen to his mother, and she did not want him around us. We were up in Toronto at the Hawk's Nest and [Maxine Brown, who Bernie was playing with,] was

Funkadelic in concert (with George Clinton writhing onstage).

playing on the same street, so I went down to the club when we were on break and asked Bernie to come and sit in with us. He came, sat in, and George asked him if he was interested in getting with us. Bernie gave Maxine notice, was with us a month later. We kept Tawl 'cause I knew he could play guitar, and I saw how some of the rock groups had that rhythm guitar in there. Well, with me, Bernie, and Tawl holding that rhythm down, Eddie had a field day.

THE PEAK

We had straight-up crossover [appeal]. People knew it. Norman Whitfield would bring his tape recorder to the Twenty Grand and record our shows. I put a stop to that. One particular time, Norman came and I seen him get out of his car in the parking lot and cue his recorder up. By that time, "Cloud 9" and "I Can't Get Next to You" were out, and he was definitely taking our groove. I went out of the club: "Norman, please don't bring that in here. You got enough, man." He started cussin' me out and all that. So I went straight to the club manager's office, told the security guard at the front door and they held him up. He tried to lie, but they searched him and found it. So me and Norman didn't get along for a long time, said he was gonna fuck me up and all that. The gangsters told him if a hair gets touched on my head—"That's a Funkadelic; he can't do no wrong. Besides, you shouldn't've got busted."

We started doing TV shows like the *Upbeat*. Each time we did it, we got wilder and wilder, and [finally] got kicked off. Everyone came out on the stage wearing a diaper; that shit was fucked up. [*laughs*] I tried to tell those muthafuckas, man; they wasn't hearing me. The diaper was my idea: I used to come out in a diaper, pickaninny braids, my Vietnam or WWII combat boots, and sometimes my Eisenhower jacket. Also, had a whole bunch of medals on that Calvin didn't want that he gave me. That was my protest to Vietnam. That's where George got his idea for *America Eats Its Young*, by how I dressed.

The shit was really starting to take off when we hit England in '71. The government tried to keep us out based on the title of the album. Then they went a step further and said "Eulogy and Light" was sacrilege. But we almost got deported for that donkey shit. Like we told the donkey to come up on one of their most treasured monuments and take a shit? That was George's fucked-up idea, 'cause of the title of the album—*Free Your Mind...And Your Ass Will Follow*—to have a jackass in a picture with us. We take pictures and then when we leave there's a big pile of shit left on the steps, man. [*laughs*] When they seen that shit all over Royal Albert Hall, it was in all the papers. And American niggers at that? If we'd done something like that at Buckingham Palace, we'd've got shot. They would've put us in jail and swallowed the key.

We went in every nook and cranny, from the south all the way to the top. We did a couple of beautiful gigs in London's famous club, the Speakeasy. Everybody checked us out: Paul McCartney, George Harrison, Elton John, Santana, Jimmy Page, Ginger Baker, the Who—that was some weird shit. The only ones who weren't entertainers were some of them fabulous women they had in there. We were a little too funky for them. It was just like a big party! I was kicking at that point, taking methadone. I wasn't trying to get high. This was something monumental in our career—didn't want to [be] all fucked on heroin. We were supposed to play for the queen. We lost that gig.

SUPER STUPID

The albums? What about 'em? Rock, R&B, gospel, funk. Elements of heavy metal, acid rock too. Each album was recorded during a different session. The killer was the fact [that] we got no publishing. On *Funkadelic*, I didn't play on all those tracks. "Mommy, What's a Funkadelic?": Bob Babbitt on bass; "I'll Bet You": Jamerson. But *Free Your Mind* and *Maggot Brain* was just us. My favorite songs? All of them! But I lean toward "Super Stupid," "Funky Dollar Bill," "Hit It and Quit It," "Wars of Armageddon." "Super Stupid"—I came up with that all day long. Eddie's singing lead, like Jimi Hendrix but different. We were as psychedelic—in the same book, but on a different page. We're more R&B tinged, 'cause you can hear horn lines doin' that lick, very bluesy, but by no means is it R&B.

"Friday Night, August 14th" is our interpretation of "Foxy Lady." The lead is me and Fuzzy. Tawl sang on "Free Your Mind," "Back in our Minds," "Funky Dollar Bill." "Maggot Brain" is Eddie feeding off the spirit of what Tiki and me were giving him, but George mixed my shit down so you can't hear it. And that *Maggot Brain* cover was bullshit, satanical to say the least. Got a woman buried in the dirt up to her head, and on the back, a picture of her skull. And then the liner notes were from the Process Church of the Final Judgment—the church of Satan. That's George sabotaging us again. I didn't mind the *Free Your Mind* cover, though, 'cause she was gorgeous; that's where the Ohio Players got that.

It's okay to be bad boys of rock and roll, but look at how much class the Stones had with it. Then there's the other point of: wait, don't go too far with it; we're not White. There are things we cannot get away with because we're Black. But George didn't care about none of that, at our expense. Then when he did get a chance to do Parliament, it was spankin' clean, straight-up dance music; not Motown but the next step. But Funkadelic was straight up X-rated. He wanted to keep Funkadelic dirty, keep some semblance of control when he realized *we* were truly up for the down stroke. We were setting the trend, not the damn Parliaments.

FUNKADELIC EATS ITS YOUNG

Tawl wasn't really tryin' to leave; he just never made it back. Wasn't fair what happened. They just left him.[8] Tiki left next. Might've had something to do with drugs. Plus, I believe he was seeing Chaka Khan at the time and didn't want to be missing out on that. When he stepped, that left a hole. Got with Miles for a minute, but they were too much alike. A few years later, he was dead.[9] So when they got Tyrone Lampkin, I was done. I liked him as a person, but he did not fit the bill for our music. Harold Beane didn't fit neither. Bad mismatch. That live CD they put out from Meadowbrook is the worst. That's not the *real* Funkadelic.[10]

George used intimidation and any other tactics he could to get Funkadelic to break up. He was glad when we broke up, 'cause it made it better for him to claim all royalties and money. Then, once the original Funkadelic was out of the picture, he could concentrate on doing the same to the Parliaments. And now [the Parliaments] know I was right. It really hurts me to my heart, man. I don't take any fucking consolation in that whatsoever. It's just a pity. Could've been wonderful for all of us, but [was] literally destroyed because of selfishness, greed, ignorance, and hatin' each other. For anybody to say that wasn't the deal, they don't know what they're talking about, 'cause that's exactly what took place in Parliament-Funkadelic, man.

I'll be straight up: that's how niggers do shit. They don't *ever* stick together. If all the Beatles were alive, you can count on a reunion some day. Look at the Rolling Stones, Zeppelin—mainly, the White groups. When you start trying to put original Black groups together, there's *going…to…be… some…shit.* They might come together once, but they're not into sticking together, no matter what the odds are. Can't stand to see one make it! And then the kick in the head is the denial of it all. Parliament and Funkadelic are the epitome of that. And it all came from within. No one came in and infiltrated. One hundred percent from the inside.

———————○———————

CODA

After leaving, Billy toured for several years supporting many acts, including (with other members of Funkadelic) Ruth Copeland (opening for Sly and the Family Stone for two years), Chairmen of the Board, and the Love Machine. He also lay the fat bottom on a number of hits for other groups, such as the Commodores ("I Feel Sanctified"), Chairmen of the Board with Sly Stone ("Finder's Keepers"), the Temptations ("Shakey Ground"), Lenny Williams, the Undisputed Truth, as well as for the classic scene in Car Wash in which Richard Pryor gets his shoes shined. He released a now out-of-print funk rock solo album *O.G. Funk* in '94, and, in the same year, finally returned to the P-Funk fold to prove his Funkadelic chops before leaving again in 2004. Always looking for a gig, Billy can be reached at ogbassman@yahoo.com. ●

Notes

1. Check out "Can You Get to That," "Some More," "Eulogy and Light," "There Is Nothing Before Me but Thang," "Biological Speculation," "I Misjudged You."
2. The Boyce brothers were at the time the Parliaments' backup band.
3. Notorious New Jersey record producer/label exec.
4. Other bass influences: "Paul McCartney, Larry Graham, Jerry Jemmott."
5. Drum company; also slang for a fiberglass (and usually heavy-sounding) drum kit.
6. Parliament's *Osmium*.
7. Saxophonist Herbert ("Sparky") Sparkman had joined Funkadelic and recorded vocals on "Music for My Mother."
8. For more details of this incident, check CD booklet to Funkadelic compilation, *Music for Your Mother*.
9. Billy says, "His funeral was sad and extremely to the real. Died of cancer. We were in L.A., he was horsing around with some friends, slipped on the grass and broke his hip. When they operated on him they found cancer in his hip. He was only in his early thirties."
10. Funkadelic, *Live: Meadowbrook, Rochester, Michigan, 12th September, 1971*. Harold Beane and Tyrone Lampkin had just joined the band.

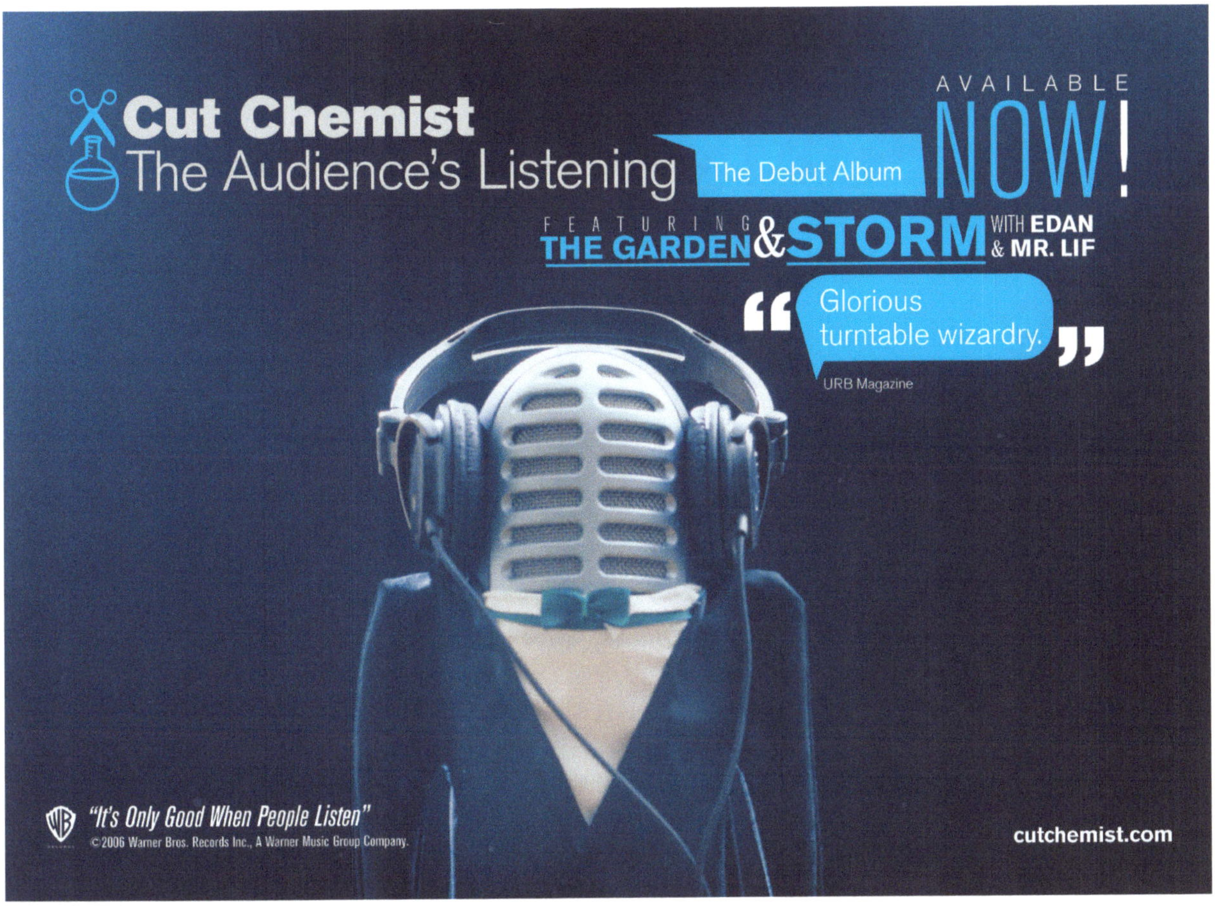

Cut Chemist
The Audience's Listening
The Debut Album
AVAILABLE
NOW!
FEATURING THE GARDEN & STORM WITH EDAN & MR. LIF
"Glorious turntable wizardry."
URB Magazine
"It's Only Good When People Listen"
©2006 Warner Bros. Records Inc., A Warner Music Group Company.
cutchemist.com

music is my art
HVW8
ART · MUSIC LOS ANGELES · MONTREAL
661 N. SPAULDING, 90046
GALLERY · STORE · STUDIO
HEAVYWEIGHT PRODUCTION HOUSE · EST. 1998 · WWW.HVW8.COM

MAGIC BOOTH #ST30620-19
MIXER FRIENDLY
POSITIVE APPAREL
YA DIG?
RE·BOP
DJ SMASH
Mobile Global
Blue Note, Savoy
FALL COLLECTION 2006
415.846.8397
orders@mixerfriendly.com
www.mixerfriendly.com

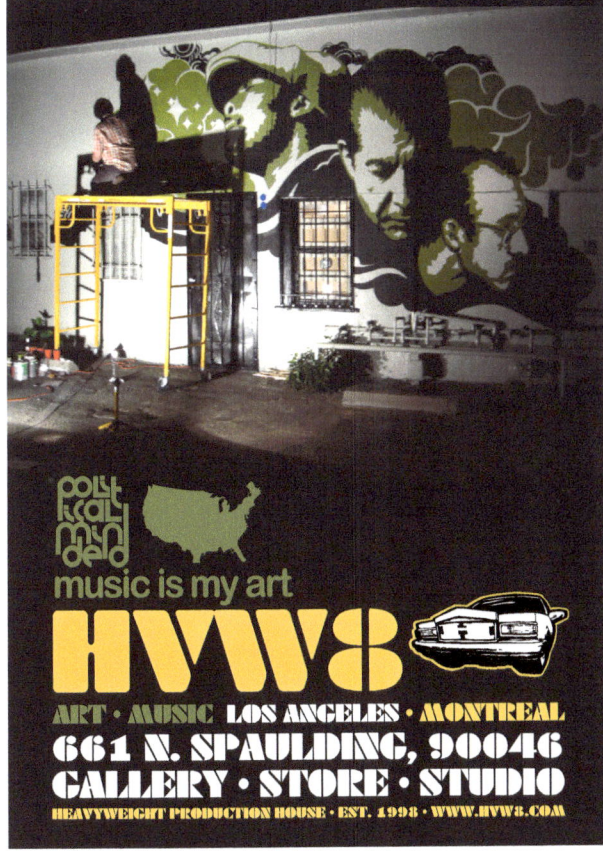

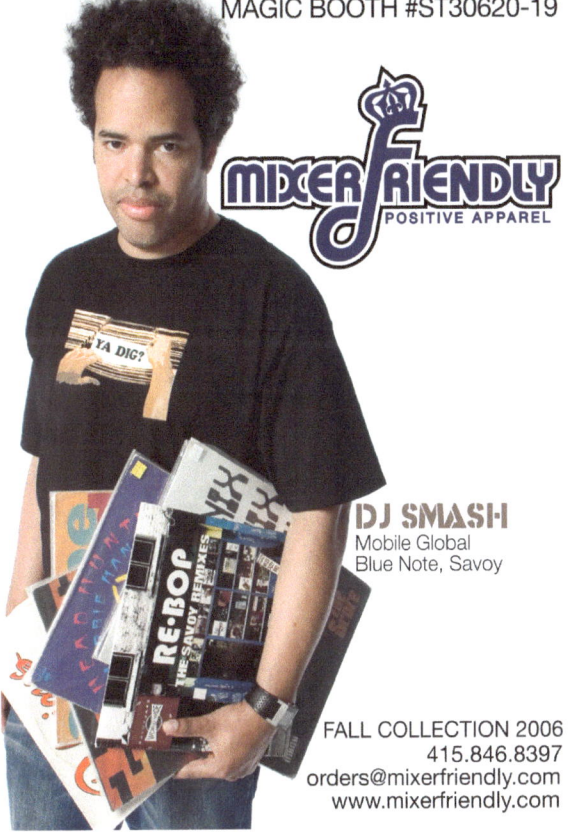

coming this fall

CATCH AS CATCH CAN

check out glue on tour this fall with the sol-illaquists of sound in a city near you

sept 05 @ drunken unicorn - atlanta, ga
sept 06 @ awful arthur's towers - roanoke, va
sept 07 @ ottobar - baltimore, md
sept 08 @ first unitarian church - philadelphia, pa
sept 09 @ knitting factory - new york, ny
sept 11 @ living room - providence, ri
sept 12 @ great scott - allston, ma
sept 14 @ higher ground - burlington, vt
sept 19 @ magic stick - detroit, mi
sept 21 @ rhino's - bloomington, in
sept 22 @ abbey pub - chicago, il
sept 28 @ belly up - aspen, co

sept 29 @ larimer lounge - denver, co
sept 30 @ black sheep - colorado springs, co
oct 01 @ kayo gallery - salt lake city, ut
oct 04 @ the loft - missoula, mt
oct 05 @ chop suey - seattle, wa
oct 06 @ holocene - portland, or
oct 07 @ wow hall - eugene, or
oct 09 @ bottom of the hill - san francisco, ca
oct 13 @ big fish pub - tempe, az
oct 17 @ emo's - austin, tx
oct 19 @ beta bar - tallahassee, fl

for more information visit www.gluemakesmusic.com www.myspace.com/glue www.fatbeats.com and www.myspace.com/fatbeatsrecords

in stores now

louis logic & j.j. brown
misery loves comedy

ugly duckling
bang for the buck

el da sensei
the unusual

coming soon: new albums from akrobatik, black milk, count bass d, one be lo, pseudo slang and more

The Wax Poetics and Phase 2
Limited Edition T-shirt.

Visit waxpoetics.com for this and other Wax Poetics merchandise.

THE SYNTHESIZER

BERNIE WORRELL WAS THE KEY TO THE PARLIAMENT-FUNKADELIC SOUND

by Matt Rogers • photos courtesy of Bernie and Judie Worrell

"Dr. Dre should have a holiday for Bernie Worrell." —Mos Def
"Bernie is like a genius of geniuses." —George Clinton

"Bernie, on this pass, can you give me that same soulful shit but with a bit more of a classical feel? Sure, more arpeggio but not fast." The track begins: thudding dub bass, elastic synth lines, a melodica's floating note, and the frosting now being added, a Bernie Worrell harpsichord solo, which scurries forth like a beach crab from under a rock. Goofy grins paste the faces of Prince Paul and Don Newkirk, who are perched behind the soundboard in the engineer's control room of Lenny Kravitz's midtown studio, watching the former child prodigy get loose. A few hours earlier, Yellowman had stopped by to gild his signature voice onto this same "reggae" track that is morphing, no doubt, into some uniquely twisted shit. But what the hell else would you expect from a collaboration between a Handsome Boy and a Woo Warrior?

"There's perfect pitch and absolute pitch. I was born with perfect pitch," this founding father of funk informs me. "That means you could tap on a piece of metal and I'll tell you what pitch it is. I'll hear a jet flying overhead and tell you what frequency, tone, pitch it is." So if you find yourself talking with Bernie, don't take it personally if he suddenly seems distracted by something you can't hear. Don't blame him for blurting out the keys or pitches emanating from birds chatting near or far. The man simply can't help it. He also can't help mastering any keyboard put before him. Name it, chances are he's tamed it: piano, Hammond organ, pipe organ, Farfisa, Rhodes, Clavinet, Wurlitzer, RMI, melodica, Moog, ARP, Yamaha, and many more; the man is a virtual grab bag of keyboard wizardry. In fact, as one might with Herbie Hancock or the late Billy Preston, you could almost trace the evolution of the electronic keyboard via this one man. A man that enabled Parliament-Funkadelic and every resultant P-Funk baby (be it Bootsy's Rubber Band, the Brides, Parlet, or the Horny Horns), like no mob before them, bum-rush any musical genre they pleased. A man that helped bring serious props to the Talking Heads and gave folks like De La Soul, Ice Cube, Dr. Dre, and Snoop Dogg (who calls him "Uncle Bernie") endless fodder to change popular music forever.

Moreover, a dynamic list of who he's recorded with outside of said universes is plain stupefying: Fela, Tony Williams, Mtume, Pharoah Sanders, Manu Dibango, Johnnie Taylor, Jack Bruce, Ginger Baker, Buddy Guy, Yoko Ono, and on and on. Simply put, Bernie Worrell lives to play music, whether it's recording a melodica-only record for a Japanese label, spazzing out with Mos Def's Black Jack Johnson, making featured spot appearances with George Clinton's current P-Funk posse, or pushing his own band, the Woo Warriors (which includes Derrick Davis, son of Raymond Davis, on bass), who with their own brand of funk can hit it and quit it like a heart attack. Yet, why does it seem so many people are still sleeping on one of the most underrated musicians of his generation? A soon-to-be released documentary, *Stranger: Bernie Worrell on Earth*, tries to answer that very question by asking several musical heavyweights who have lived a while in Bernie's Woo-niverse. Bernie would much rather play music than talk about it, but he was kind enough to let us try anyway.

"I didn't know music; all I could tell Bernie is I wanna see green; he could interpret it to damn near precisely what I was saying." —George Clinton

BERNIE WORRELL: I was a child prodigy. My mom showed me a scale on the piano when I was three and I played it back: then I was gone. I was born with a gift: perfect pitch. My first concert was at four years old. I wrote my first piano concerto at eight and played three piano concertos with the Washington Symphony Orchestra at ten years old. I played forty classical pieces up through twelfth grade. I'm sixty-two now and been playing for fifty-nine years. I can play anything.

My mom, of course, wanted me to be a classical pianist.

(*opposite*) Bernie Worrell playing the melodica, circa late '70s. Photo by Judie Worrell.

She had a beautiful voice, was a vocalist in the church, and she would accompany herself. My father was a truck driver; my mother a domestic worker. We moved to Plainfield [from Long Branch] when I was eight years old. My teacher was Ms. Fay Barnaby Kent, a Quaker lady. Her teacher was one of the first American composers: Edward MacDowell. My mom used to clean her house, and that's how lessons happened. I was, like, her favorite. I would pass all her college students—I was twelve—and be the highlight of her recitals, the only Black kid there. [*laughs*] I was also the pipe organist for the Episcopalian church (my mom would go there too), then I'd accompany my mom at her church—Shiloh Baptist—when she had a solo, and when she sang at fashion shows and teas in town. So I played pipe organ for the Episcopalians, Hammond organ for the Baptists, and then piano for her little shows. I was raised Catholic, and was in the chancellor choir at the Catholic church. One day I heard "Rockin' Charlie"—a piano instrumental—and I started playing that over and over. Then, listening to R&B radio stations in my room, anything I heard I could play.

I went to see the Parliaments at a grammar school and a local roller rink. I managed to get out of the house to see that. See, I used to sneak out of my bedroom window and go down to the barbershop and get my hair processed. My mom was strict; she wouldn't let me hang out on the street corners with "the hoodlums" as [she] would call them. "You're not going down to the barbershop with George Clinton!" Sometimes she would follow with switches and switch me out of the barber chair and switch George. [*laughs*] The Parliaments were also barbers, and the barbershop was a meeting place in any neighborhood, and they would be there rehearsing. Music and hair went hand in hand, I guess. They heard that this new kid came to town, heard he was "genius" material. Later on, I did some lead sheets for them, sat in—think I was still in high school. And George said, "One day when I can afford you, I'll call." That happened maybe eight years later.

After high school, I had maybe a half a year off. Had private lessons at Juilliard, then went to the New England Conservatory for Music. My piano teacher was Yugoslavian—Michelob Schwab. He taught me the wrist technique, 'cause his hands were really short, so in order to reach an octave he'd rolled his wrists, which would put you in forward motion to reach the next octave. Before college, I had had harmony and theory for about four years from Professor John F. Noge from the New York College of Music. I met him through Fay Barnaby Kent. My mother used to take me to Linden, New Jersey, every Saturday for three to four years, so when I got to college they skipped me to second year of theory. I took timpani lessons from Vic Firth from the Boston Symphony; he's a character. He liked my cousin, and I liked his wife. Anyway, I was away from home: freedom! So I went crazy; I am crazy; I like being crazy.

Since I had perfect pitch, there was some envy from other students: "How you do that?" I didn't know myself that I had it. Everyone would test me: Bernie what's this, what's that? And I could sight-read like a snap, because I would accompany all the vocal operatic majors for their promotion recitals and daily lessons during the week. I'd practice, if I could stand it, maybe three hours a day. A lot of the kids were jealous, 'cause they'd be in there like an eight-hour day. Not me. I'd hit the road, be hanging out in town partying, 'cause I had it in me. When I'd get to my teacher's for my weekly lesson, half the lesson, he'd say, "Play some jazz." So I'd improvise and [Schwab] was hooked.

There were about five Black students in the school at the time, but no one messed with me. I see no color except when someone messes with me. Whoever it is: Black, White, yellow, green, they're gonna hear it. The classes were a drag. But I was accompanying recitals, orchestra, playing timpani. These were side gigs to earn a little money. My other side jobs were accompany[ing] on Saturdays a male Jewish choir, and a French ballet teacher. And then at night, I'd play nightclubs. I didn't get in much trouble, [because] I could hear something then play it, so I was cool. Besides, the professors were lushes! When I found that out, I didn't worry too much; they were just like us. Everybody—Boston Symphony Orchestra, Boston Pops—they were all drinking; lot of alcoholics, full of *snobassery*. Hypocrites. Not just them but society. European. American. Society. Highbrow. Blue bloods. Classical thing. This is "superior"—I don't think so! I didn't like the idea of classical music being elevated above everything else. That's bullcrap.

For my club gigs, I was mostly playing in organ trios. I was part of the house band at the Basin Street South club in Roxbury. There'd be a whole show: dinner, the comedian, dancers, then the main act, which would be a vocalist or a saxophonist. So [I was] coming out of the church thing, going into the jazz and R&B organ. Organ, sax, drums, sometimes guitar, but mostly just the Hammond, 'cause the Hammond could sound like a full orchestra if you knew what you're doing. I saw Charlie Earland, the Silver Fox [Jack McDuff], Houston Person. The club would be packed, the sweat pouring. It was just invigorating. Only three pieces, but the fullness would sound like a ten-piece band. And you cut down the expenses.

My first big professional gig was with the Joe Thomas and Bill Elliot Quintet. Bill was going with Dionne [Warwick] then so I backed her. I also backed Tammi Terrell (known as Montgomery then), Freddie Scott, Tommy Hunt, Pigmeat Markham, Baby Seals, Moms Mabley, different artists that came through. Then I got hooked up with Maxine Brown. She and my mom was tight. If you were playing baby grand and organ with Maxine Brown, you knew what you're doing. She was with Chuck Jackson for a while, and they were great. I toured with Maxine for five years or so, you know, doing the chitlin circuit, and then, while we were opening for Jimmy Smith in Bermuda got a call from Judie that she was going to meet with George at the Apollo. This is around '69. So George told Judie, "Okay, I can afford Bernie now, but you're gonna have to move to Detroit." And we said, "Wow, okay." George had moved the group to Detroit. Maxine's career was on the downturn. So, went back to New York, then moved to Detroit for the first Funkadelic album. It was crazy, and the rest is history.

BERNIE'S BREAKDOWN

Other than George Clinton, Bernie Worrell is the one person who has experienced nearly all of the Parliament-Funkadelic lineups and contributed to all of the many satellite projects. So we start the rundown from the beginning and listen to a few records along the way.

The Parliaments. Let's see. Calvin Simon: lead vocalist on some songs, background, costuming, and percussion. Slick, pimp-mode. Ray Davis: lead on some songs and background. Ray [had a] voice like Paul Robeson. Aries like me; you don't tell him what to do. Sweetheart, ladies man; deep voice, slay them with that. Shy, but when he opened his mouth, they'd fall out. Clarence "Fuzzy" Haskins: my roommate, lead and background vocals, dance the sex dance on stage, wore the long johns. Gemini, energy galore, he had you laughing on the long road trips 24-7, and practical jokes, you'd have to watch your back. Grady Thomas: the *purple* man, he started purple way before my wife or Prince. Everything purple: motorcycles, clothes, *everything*. Purple and patchouli oil. He'd play percussion and drums. Mostly background [vocals]. Grady was a Capricorn, slow-moving, too slow for me, but earthy. Liked flea markets. Then you got George Clinton: writer, lead vocalist. [*laughs*] Whatever! Sage, business head, slick, y'all know the deal. George's favorite singers were Smoky Robinson and Anthony Newly, the English balladeer. [*laughs*]

The Funkadelics. Billy "Bass" Nelson, the original Funkadelic bass player. Lots of vibe, very intelligent. George would have a lot of his arguments with Billy; he'd never quit. Eddie Hazel: guitar. The original Maggot Brain. I don't wanna say another Jimi [Hendrix] but that status, that same gift; special. He could also sing and play drums. Tawl Ross: original rhythm guitarist and vocalist. He was out there. I think the acid did it. He was a performer. His moves—Iggy Pop type of theatrics—some people called him strange back in the day. He was! Tiki Fulwood: drums. Out of Philly, was playing with, I think, the Intruders. I met him at the Apollo when I was with Maxine Brown. He was bad, full-up rock and funk, in the foot, hit hard.

On the early records, did you guys have a particular process for recording?

Whatever the process that captured the moment. A lot of times—I don't want to put it into percentages, because the percentages changed depending on whose project it was and the project's different parameters—just going in to jam captured the spontaneous thing. We'd take just a little piece of that jam into song form, maybe no lyric content at that moment. The original Funkadelics—Billy, Eddie, Tiki, and Tawl (when they let him in)—they *jammed*, you know. That shit be *bad*. George would track it, then put it together. I'd sometimes play with them, but mostly I'd be at the board putting the thing together in a format or helping with the

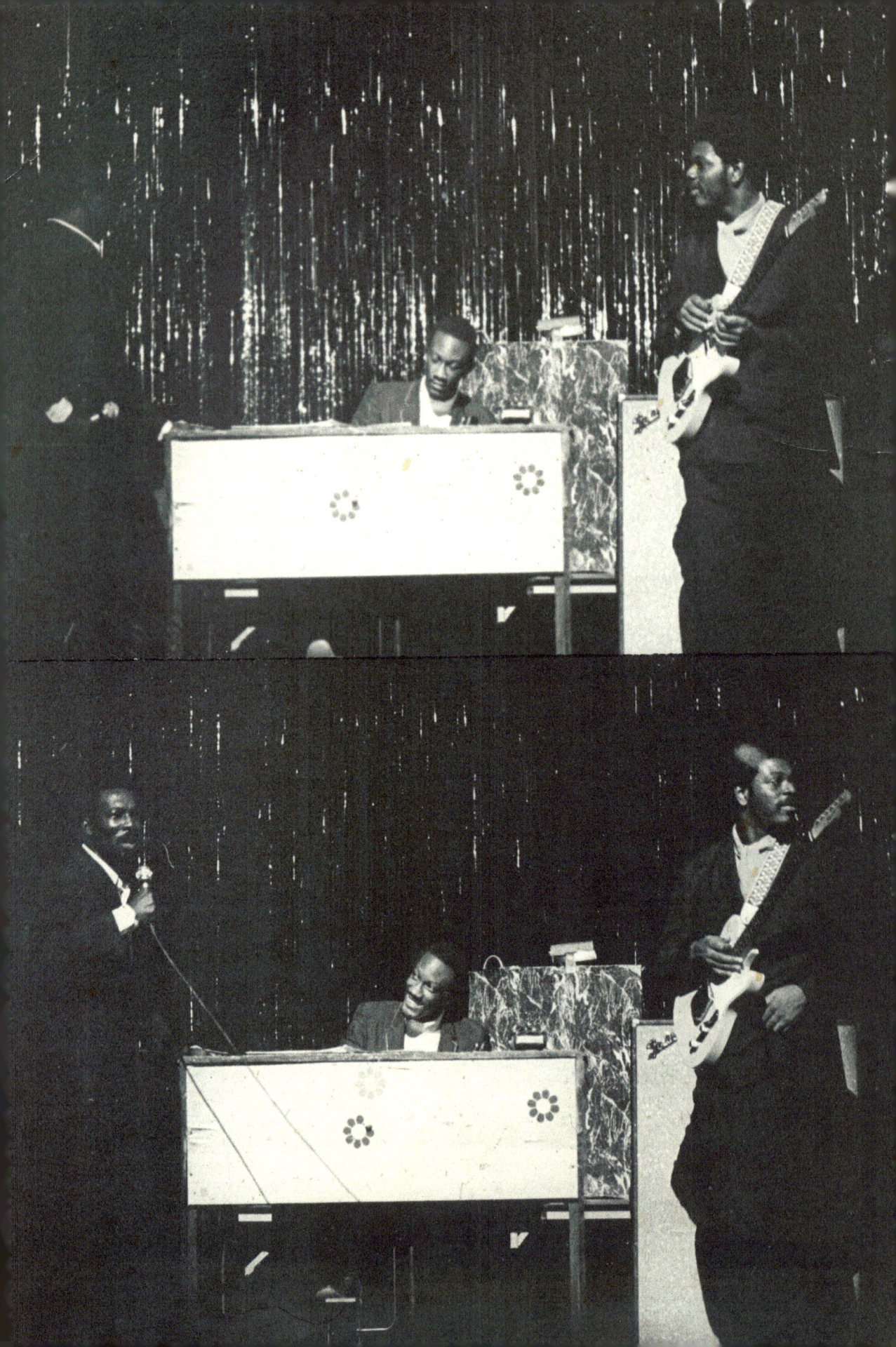

Bernie Worrell and George Clinton hangin' with the execs.

arrangement. Or, sometimes, I'd go into the recording room and George'd be inside the control room; then I'd put my parts on later. Mostly, I'd get everything together, arrangements, and whatnot, and then put my parts together, whatever was needed, so there'd be some keys with the rest of the stuff. Then after some lyric content, we'd overdub. Then I'd put the sweetener on it. Build the track to whatever it became. George, his thing is stacking vocals; that's what Garry Shider learned [from him]. Other times maybe George or someone would say something like a chant thing, then the story line would be built later. That was usually George's department, besides melody and tempo.

Like James Brown, it seems George always managed to get songwriting credit.

[*laughs*] How'd he do that? He didn't write everything. That's 'cause Westbound and George were all tied up together. [Label owner] Armen [Boladian] won't say shit though.

You're on 1970's *Funkadelic* even though you're not credited on the original notes?

I'm playing on it, for sure. My picture is on the back. Had every instrument on the same line; you know, come up with the theme and have everyone stack up. Make it heavier, like in rock. Before that, the [Funkadelics] were just playing.

"Bernie should be credited for creating an entire language." –Bill Laswell

It's impossible to even begin to grasp the impact of Bernie's musicianship without closely listening to the entire P-Funk catalog. As the '70s wear on and overdubbing becomes prevalent, many songs are virtual conversations between Bernie and his keyboards (or, rather, himself). If you'd like to get a quick taste on this man's diverse palette, check the following:

Hammond organ: "Funky Woman," "Hit It and Quit It," "Wars of Armageddon"
RMI: "I Wanna Know If It's Good to You?," "Free Your Mind," "Loose Booty"
Acoustic piano: "Funky Dollar Bill," "Jimmy's Got a Little Bit of Bitch in Him"
Clavinet: "Joyful Process," "Up for the Down Stroke," "Red Hot Mama"
Minimoog: "Flash Light," "Aqua Boogie," "Knee Deep," "Let's Take It to the Stage"
ARP String Ensemble: "Chocolate City," "Undisco Kidd"
Harpsichord: "Oh Lord, Why Lord?"

Let's listen to some original Funkadelic.

"I Call My Baby Pussycat" *Live: Meadowbrook, 1971* **(Westbound)**

Was this the typical live sound for Funkadelic then?

Sometimes we was just vamping for days and days. It would get a little tiring, but people loved it 'cause there was so much to look at. Nowadays, the audience gets tired of a forty-five-minute song. See, the outfits started because George couldn't keep anything straight. He'd be losing shit all the time—ties, shoes, socks—couldn't keep a suit clean, so he started mismatching shit, which I loved, 'cause I was coming from Maxine where you had to wear suits: that whole chitlin circuit thing. We [did] a lot of rock shows too:

(*opposite*) Bernie Worrell (on organ) sitting in with Wilson Pickett (on the mic) and his guitarist, likely at the Apollo circa the late '60s, before joining Funkadelic.

MC5, Mitch Ryder and Detroit Wheels, Bob Seger, Alice Cooper. That started the cult following. That's when George was stripping and crazy hairdos and acid: Funkadelic.

Any other Black band doing that at the time?

No, we were taking it a little further. Audience was White, and they didn't want that shit over the airwaves or live in front of their White ladies. George'd just be wearing a sheet and barefoot with moons and stars cut in his head. [*laughs*] We played a lot of dates with Ted Nugent. That's the wild man, a hunter like George. Him and George, the wild boys, would go hunting together.

"Free Your Mind and Your Ass Will Follow" *Free Your Mind...* (Westbound) 1970

This is Tawl [on vocals], with Tiki doing the high part. Crazy thing Tawl. "Free of the need to be free." [That's] the concept. Everyone trying to be free, well, you *are*. That's the RMI [Rocky Mountain Instruments Electra-piano]—pre-Moog—I'm playing the whole song. Before, I'd play a lot of Hammond, but then the RMI came out: had piano, organ, harpsichord, flute on it, and you could mix the combinations. I heard Stevie [Wonder] bought the first, so I got the second one in Detroit. Everybody thought I was playing synthesizer.

"Maggot Brain" *Maggot Brain* (Westbound) 1971

This makes me cry. Where'd he get the idea? [Eddie] was probably hiding up somewhere; George be fucking with him, calling him names, or he might've been arguing with him (we all argued with George) and started calling Eddie "Maggot Brain," that his brain [was] turning to jelly. So he probably went to the studio feeling that way; I think we recorded this at A&R Studios in NYC. "Funky Dollar Bill" was also cut there.

"Funky Dollar Bill" *Free Your Mind...*

Yeah, this is the shit here. Yeah, Eddie! [*laughs*] That's Tawl leading this [on vocals]. Distinctive, ain't it? Like Iggy. [*crazy piano runs*] Oh shit, I've got the solo here too. I used the upright piano with the attacks on the hammers. See, I'm free. I do what I want. That just happens by magic—the rhythm picking up with the piano. We'd do this live too; it'd be a little more raggedy but… Someone ought to do this over again. I know who: Robert Randolph would kill this.

"Hit It and Quit It" *Maggot Brain*

Ahh yeah, I arranged this. I'm doing lead [vocals]; I don't tell nobody. I just started doing it again with the Woo Warriors. It jumps in on the "off" beat. They couldn't get the right intro, 'cause the accent was *here*. [*laughs*] My patience was going with them. I'm playing the line on the organ—that's an example of everybody on the same line. Oops, that was a mistake. [*laughs*] They messed the chord up. I try to teach them the chords; sometimes they get it. This was psychedelics mixed with funk. I arranged those backup vocals. We just messed around, and George said, "Fuck it, hit it and quit it, next!"

"Super Stupid" *Maggot Brain*

Ahh shit, yeah. This is about Eddie, this is all him, and all the Funkadelics snorting heroin. It's about us, just super stupid. That's Eddie singing lead—yeah baby! Zeppelin! And I put this in [*short organ bridge*] to set up the solo. Here we go! Zeppelin! Those congas might've been Eddie "Bongo" [Brown] from Motown.

"Wars of Armageddon" *Maggot Brain*

Oh shoot, damn, this is bad too. That [Armageddon] is what was getting ready to happen. Billy and Tiki jamming.

Kind of has that Miles Davis feel at the time.

Oh, well, he was listening to us. Someone was telling me years later that Miles was trying to find me; he wanted me to take somebody's place. I met Miles a couple of times. Miles took Tiki. There was a jazz club in Boston called Paul's Mall, which I played with Maxine, across from Jazz Workshop—it's not there anymore—on Boylston Street. Miles was at the Jazz Workshop, we were at Paul's Mall which was unusual; P-Funk at Paul's Mall? *O-kay*! So we had just come off and Miles walked in, stood in the middle of the doorway, didn't say a word, just stared. You know those eyes of his when he stared at you; that shit go right through you. Ain't nobody say nothing. He just looked, then turned and left. Next day, Tiki was gone! He went with Miles [*laughs*] but he came back, off and on.

"It's like Jimi Hendrix on keyboards." –Bootsy

Around this point in time (circa '72 and *America Eats Its Young*), a slew of musicians join the Parliament-Funkadelic collective, recording (credited and uncredited) under Funkadelic and then, a little later, Parliament, setting in motion the satellite groups like the Rubber Band and Brides of Funkenstein, that will develop throughout the remainder of the decade. Bernie has both hands in all of them.

Things begin to blow up and you are there for it all. Let's quickly talk about some of the main players by instrument.

Drums

Tyrone Lampkin: out of Conneticut, took over when Tiki left. Tyrone was brought up in jazz, Broadway, funk; he could play all styles. His technique was fluid, came from marching bands along with the funk, jazz. Jerome Brailey: "Bigfoot." Met him before P-Funk when he was with Chambers Brothers, then with the Five Stairsteps, on "O-o-h Child," which you still hear today. He was funky, light touch, heavy on the foot. Then Dennis Chambers: he was a monster. Out of Baltimore. He and Rodney "Skeet" Curtis on bass, they came together. Phenomenal. Last I heard he's with Santana. Bootsy [also] played drums, and of course Frankie "Kash" [Waddy].

Bass

Cordell "Boogie" Mosson: came with Garry Shider. Libra. Boogie had a special style, just felt good, was more bouncy. Billy'd stay on the bottom, be down on it, more rock-like lines. Boogie'd move around more. Similar to Bootsy. Bootsy played a bit off the beat. [He] brought the J.B.'s discipline and the comedy, cartoon thing. When I was doing Bootsy's camp, it was more organized than P-Funk. The guys admired their structure and discipline. Prakash John: Indian brother. Ladies loved him. From Alice Cooper, Lou Reed. Then "Skeet" Curtis: a whiz, jazz phenomenon; he could play anything. Oh, then this guy Bernie Worrell: keyboard bass.

Guitar

P-Funk in concert, circa early '70s.

Harold Beane: out of Memphis, from Isaac Hayes and that Memphis Stew feel. R&B background. Ron Bykowski: our Polish cohort out of Detroit. He and Eddie did a version of "Cosmic Slop" together. Ron was master of feedback, could hold it for days. Catfish: all the rhythm, discipline. He wouldn't move; that shit'd be there in the pocket. Catfish wasn't so much with P-Funk, but was a vital part with the Rubber Band. Practical joker like Fuzzy, ladies' man, liked his alcohol, but his business straight. He had had it after the Rubber Band, couldn't be bothered with all the shit. Shider and Boogie also play guitar. Then Mike Hampton: that's Kidd Funkadelic. He's forty-something now but we got him when he was eighteen; had to learn "Maggot Brain" note for note. Little baby genius. Big shoes to fill and he did it. Blackbyrd McKnight: was with Herbie Hancock and the Headhunters. West Coast, L.A. Phenomenal, can play anything. Great person, of course; Aries—two days before me. Kick ass. Who else? Too many….

Horns

Fred and Maceo, more J.B. influence with the P-Funk sound. Another emergence, another arm, another limb from the tree. They brought trumpeters Rick Gardner and [Richard] "Kush" Griffith. Then that shit was *funky*!

Vocalists, Women

Mallia Franklin, Debbie Wright, Jeanette Washington—Parlet. Then my babies—Brides of Funkenstein—Lynn Mabry and Dawn Silva. Lynn was Sly Stone's cousin. We met them in Baltimore at the Convention Center; Sly opened for us, and then they were over here. They did all background for Parliament-Funkadelic, then their own sessions [and] Junie's albums. The Brides were more polished like Parliament, whereas Parlet was more raw like Funkadelic. "Disco to Go." Both of them were hot. I'd take both groups to go!

Vocalists, Men

Garry Shider: church you know. Damn, can't forget that voice, in his younger days. Glenn Goins: absolutely incredible. Church. Larry Heckstall: the original Sir Nose. Junie Morrison: came when Ohio Players broke up. Monster producer, songwriter, arranger, vocalist, keyboardist. I welcomed [him], 'cause it freed me up.

By 1975, you guys are recording under Funkadelic, Parliament, and Bootsy's Rubber Band, adding the J.B. horns. It was a real party.

Yeah, it was a circus, but George loved it. He loved the chaos—something going on all the time. Up to forty people on stage. Including techs: fifty. It was crazy. Too many for my liking!

How was it kept together?

[*laughs*] I don't know! I didn't get into that. Be on the bus, plane, hotel, house, whatever, on time. I was musical director and bandleader, that's it.

How did you direct?

I could hear everything. I'd give cues with my head.

For the rookies out there, how would you sum up the main differences between Parliament and Funkadelic?

Funkadelic was very raw, heavy, intense, more rock. Parliament was slick, more horns, a little more funk.

Bernie working out at his gym, 2006. Photo by Matt Rogers.

Let's listen to some more music.
Parliament "Up for the Down Stroke" *Up for the Down Stroke* **(Casablanca) 1974**

I did the primary arrangements on the whole thing, wrote all the charts, the horns, and basic rhythm track. That's the Detroit horns with Fred and Maceo. Bootsy's on bass. Heavy. Hear that? Climbing up above the bass: *dah dah dah dah*. That's the clavinet going through the wah-wah. I like the mix on this. Lots of clavinet!

Funkadelic "Loose Booty" *America Eats Its Young* **(Westbound) 1973**

That's me on the RMI; sounds like a synth. [*laughs*] [George] is messing around with everyone.

Was "loose booty" slang for anything?

For "junkie." [*Bernie wobbles a bit*] Loose, wobbly. [*laughs*] He was talking 'bout everyone; muthafuckas were loose—male, female—loose butt, so I played like I was loose, drunk, all over the place. Hey, there's "Pop Goes the Weasel." I can do different combinations of songs within the song—enjoy doing that. That's Boogie on bass there.

Funkadelic "Standing on the Verge of Getting It On" *Standing on the Verge of Getting It On* **(Westbound) 1974**

During the live shows, this was bad. That guitar is bad. That's Boogie on bass. Hear the difference? He's an Air sign. Billy'd be more in the rock, funk, heavy; that heroin tempo. This here is the cocaine tempo. We were doing the coke—Parliament. Funkadelic was more heroin.

Parliament "Mothership Connection (Star Child)" *Mothership Connection* **(Casablanca) 1976**

That's the connection, the whole theme, the whole everything right there. We coming at you from every angle. This put us over the top. I'm playing at least five different keyboards on this one.

Funkadelic "(Not Just) Knee Deep" *Uncle Jam Wants You* **(Warner Bros.) 1979**

Junie Morrison and me. I believe we were both playing keys at the same time. Acoustic piano, doing the Minimoog bass line, and Junie's doing it as well. That's why it's so heavy. We were always on the same wavelength, and with the vocals, that put the icing on the cake. Put *more* icing on it anyway, 'cause there was already plenty there. We got the sugar, but it won't harm you.

All these ensembles going on and you seemed to have hands in all of them. Talk about working with the Rubber Band.

The process was more organized but we'd jam also, 'cause they were influenced by P-Funk. Main writers were George, Bootsy, and myself. Used P-Funk personnel and then Maceo and Fred Wesley. Backgrounds would be Shider and some of the Brides. [Gary] "Mudbone" [Cooper] would sing the leads, and [Robert] "Peanut" [Johnson], mostly. Wild and crazy character.

Bootsy's Rubber Band "I'd Rather Be with You" *Stretchin' Out in Bootsy's Rubber Band* **(Warner Bros.) 1976**

You have that great melodica line in this.

Thank you. Mudbone was a classic vocalist. His sound is one of the most important factors in this song. This man could (can) sing. And you hear Bootsy's bass sound in this. It is so big! And wet! And you can quote that. Bootsy: big and wet! [*laughs*]

Bernie Worrell and Jerry Harrison of the Talking Heads, circa the early '80s.

And you start performing for a more African American crowd, as the funk festivals start to take off.

Went from White to mixed to all Black. Word spread, the cult thing snowballed, then came the Asians, and then different generations, all nations, all colors. The Blacks were as closed-minded as the Whites. Each group had their cynicism, racism, prejudices; we all got it. Funk was a bad word, and now everybody uses it. I remember George and Bootsy saying, "Watch, one day, they"—whoever they was—"gonna take it." Now look. [For a while] it was underground. Except for James Brown. He didn't like George at all. James wanted nothing to do with us. George made fun of him in "Let's Take It to the Stage." Everybody really [e.g. "Earth, Hot Air and No Fire"].

"What would life be on Earth without 'Flash Light?'"
—Mos Def

Around the mid- to late '70s, you really started using the Minimoog.

"Flash Light" sealed the deal on that instrument.

Well, I know you get asked about it all the time, but I gotta ask... So that bass on "Flash Light" is all Minimoog?

I'm playing everything on this except drums, guitar, and vocals. I'm playing all the keys, I don't think there's a clavinet on it. There are at least four Minimoogs I'm using—all set differently to give that different thick bass sound—and I'm using the ARP String Ensemble.

The Gap Band stood behind me at a show, saw how I was doing the Minimoog, then they came out with their hits. Stevie had the larger model. Keith Emerson, my baby—his *Tarkus* is still one of my favorite albums.

Any shows in particular stick out for you?

When we sold out the L.A. Forum, that was the first real recognition. I saw a sea of cars and people in limos riding back to our hotel after sound check—damn. Sold out Madison Square Garden three times. We could go to D.C., the Capitol Center, and sell out every few months. Philly, the Spectrum.

And the funk festivals?

Chaos! Crazy. Getting high, chattin' up a chick—that sounds English—sleeping wherever, getting contacts, watching bands. Play, next! We were tight with the Ohio Players, Sly, Bar-Kays, Mandrill—real tight. Chaka Khan, Rufus. Brothers Johnson—we had to take them under our wing, 'cause they'd fight like Ginger Baker and Jack Bruce. Earth, Wind and Fire were sort of like our rivals after we wore 'em out. One show we went on first; after we finished, supposedly Verdine said to Maurice, "We can't follow that." Sometimes we preferred to go on first, then get out of there. We didn't give a shit, 'cause we were the mob, the Funk Mob, Uncle Jam's Army. [*laughs*] No real rivalry. What they gonna do? Get their ass kicked. And the music and the vibe would back it up. Come on, try it!

Then you had your first solo record, 1978's *All the Woo in the World*, that has "Insurance Man for the Funk."

I didn't really want to do [a solo album], but they persuaded me. George says it's his favorite of all of mine. That and the Laswell-coproduced *Blacktronic Science*. To me, it's *ehhh*—nice. I know "Insurance Man for the Funk" is now considered a classic; it's a classic, with jazz flavorings. I get people asking me all the time to start playing it again, so I might add it to the set. But I don't know. I like *Blacktronic Science*; that's my favorite. Bill Laswell hooked that one up; he had the idea. I knew both of them [Maceo Parker and Tony Williams], of course, from before, but I was afraid to play with Tony. I used to play in the organ house band with Tony's father, T. Williams, when I was in college. He was the saxophonist. I met Tony then. He was around nineteen then. And bad.

"If you could stick a microphone in the Milky Way, that's what you're gonna get: Bernie Worrell. It's not a key, not a scale, not a mode; it's life in the universe." —Will Calhoun

The '80s rolled in and the whole P-Funk thing basically collapsed. Time for you to move on.

I finally left in the early '80s, 'cause P-Funk was crazy, all over the place. Got complicated with George. Tired of the shit. I was doing sessions and got a call from Jerry Harrison; I didn't know who the Talking Heads were. Went to Sigma Sounds [NYC], listened to some, and I liked it. I went with the Talking Heads for about four years. I did, what, three albums and the movie [*Stop Making Sense*]. See, they used to sneak into P-Funk shows while they were still art students in Providence. I basically brought part of the band with me so that they would sound good—help Tina [Weymouth] and all them out with the instruments. They knew who to call.

What was their vibe?

Stiff! No rhythm, man. [*laughs*] That's why they hired five Black extras: Alex Weir on guitar, I brought Lynn Mabry, Dollette McDonald, Steve Scales from Tina Turner, and Busta Jones on bass to supplement Tina, give her a funky sound till she got better, and then we brought in Adrian Belew. Awesome.

What were your audiences like?

Again, mostly White, depending where in the country. Then the Blacks started coming. We kicked the Police's ass in Montreal once. The Police were headlining. They were bickering, trying to get us to go on early. One of them was saying nasty things about David, 'cause he's the nervous-in-the-corner type. It was a full moon and cloud covered, so I said, "Wait, we aren't going on yet. Wait till the moon opens up." Cloud cover passed. "Now! Hit it." We hit the stage and kicked their ass.

You've done (still do) many recording sessions. Which are some you remember the most?

Let's see. Sessions: double scale—I charge everybody that. There were all those from the Holland-Dozier-Holland stable. I was still with P-Funk. Chairmen of the Board, "Finders Keepers"—that's me on the clavinet. Freda Payne's *Band of Gold*, 100 Proof (Aged in Soul), the "Want Ads" by Honey Cone. Then there was Johnny Taylor. Oh man, Don Davis from United Sound called me, Bootsy, [and] Harold Beane. "Disco Lady." We did the arrangement. I put it together, and that sold over two million copies. I got a five-hundred-dollar bonus, and I basically wrote the cut; he wrote the melody.

Who took publishing?

Don Davis of course.

Sorry I asked.

Then Mtume, *Juicy Fruit*. Great brother, yeah! He's into the funk. I used to do a lot with him. Heath brothers were his uncles; he was hooked up. Bad. Played percussion with Miles. [Mtume] called: "Bernie, come here and sing!" I'm not much for singing, but I had a recognized falsetto tenor voice. Then I did a lot of stuff with Sly and Robbie; Yoko's solo albums; the Pretenders—Chrissy, my baby (one of them). Manu Dibango, Toure Kunde out of Africa. Then there're the Jack Bruce albums. Fela—through [Bill] Laswell, bass player out of Michigan. [Bill]'s like George, brings things together. I was introduced to him through Nona Hendryx. I was her musical director for a while. Let's see. Oh, and there was Deee-Lite. [*laughs*] They were a serious trip.

You've been sampled beyond recognition. How do you feel about that?

Well, imitation is the greatest form of flattery. But, at first, we got mad at them, then we realized it was the record companies that should've handled [all the licensing]. It's all still tied up in the courts. I've never done a session with [Dr. Dre], but then again, I did all the times he's sampled me. [*laughs*]

Last question. Was it tough for your mom when you joined P-Funk?

She came around in the end.

Visit Bernie Worrell at bernieworrell.com.

Many thanks to Judie Worrell for the good food, and to Jing-niu, Hobbes, Cochise, Kali, Sheena, Solange, and Logan for the entertainment.

All interjected quotes are taken from the documentary *Stranger: Bernie Worrell on Earth*. Visit strangermovie.com for more information.

COMIC GENIUS
ARTIST PEDRO BELL EXPLORED FUNKADELIC'S DARKER DIMENSIONS

by Edward Hill

Let's talk about why you started drawing.

Okay, my daddy seemed to be a frustrated artist. I remember, I was about age four or five when he took us to an art store and bought us some paper and pencils, and he bought *How to Draw Cartoons* and *How to Draw Landscapes*, a small assortment of books. I was surprised years later to see these books are still in art stores, so they are fifty years old.

Was there any particular comic book that influenced you?

No, because my mama, who was pretty cool on some other issues, was anti–comic book. So I never kept enough comic books around to decide if I wanted to imitate one. I did like that *Sergeant Rock* stuff. I liked the crazy overemphasized thing of, like, a guy with a bazooka blowing up a tank two hundred feet away. I learned how to draw my airplanes and tanks a little better because of that. But in terms of just going ahead and drawing comic books from scratch, I never did. Now, as far as reading, I used to read all the time, and my mama was very cool with that.

Was there anything that your parents steered you toward reading as a child.

Okay, the old man put me onto the Bible, and the parts I liked the most was the book of Genesis and the book of Revelation. With the Genesis thing, I guess I ascertained dinosaurs had to fit in somewhere, right? I got to dinosaurs from the sci-fi movies of the '50s, and that was the first thing I started drawing. And, because of the names for dinosaurs, I picked up some bits of Latin. Basically, when it's used for descriptive things, it's prefixes and suffixes in the names. Also, I studied some Latin in high school. Later on, that influence became "[Night of the] Thumpasorus [Peoples]," the P-Funk song, and later the Rumpasorus. So what I learned about Latin was later one of the components of "zeep-speak." That's what I call my slanguage that I used to write the liner notes as Sir Lleb [of Funkadelia]. I styled that after the way people like Ishmael Reed created their own versions of the English language. Or like Richard Beck, also known as Iceberg Slim, who was the first cat I was aware of who would use proper King's English and then be mofo'ing somebody in the next sentence. He was combining street terminology with proper English, which I thought was just cold! And I even learned some from [Ed] "Big Daddy" Roth, who was basically recycling what they called beatnik jargon.

Were you also into science fiction writers?

Oh yeah! I was into the classic writers like Ray Bradbury, but also new school writers like Robert Bloch and, later, Harlan Ellison, who did a lot of features in *Playboy*, back in the day. There was a company called Ace Books out of New York that just sold paperback sci-fi and fantasy books. They were only 50¢ apiece, and I could get twelve for 50¢ postage. They would print up everything from the classic people to new writers. Sometimes, they would have what they call a double issue where it's a cover on one side, but, if you turn to the back, there would be a cover on the other side, upside down, so you would get two paperback stories in one. See, the book of Genesis just spins you off into the horror movies and the sci-fi stuff! And Godzilla, the enhanced new-age dinosaur—that was my favorite dinosaur, if you want to call it one.

But my peeps influenced me in another direction of reading when I got around to asking about their participation in World War II. They met at A&M College down in Florida. The old man was on the second-string football team. Well, the army trucks rolled through and snatched off the first-string football team, and then, after he became first-string football, they snatched him off too. He got sent to the famous Tuskegee Army Air Force base where he trained as a radio operator. My mom got tired of the racist bullshit going down in Florida, so she moved up to Wisconsin and was working as a B-17 parts inspector. So when I learned all that, I started being into model airplanes, the American planes and the German stuff, and at the same time I started reading a lot of military history. So after getting into dinosaurs and WWII stuff, naturally, I was thrilled by the book of Revelation where all that wild stuff's supposed to be happening, and that's when I really started checking out all the

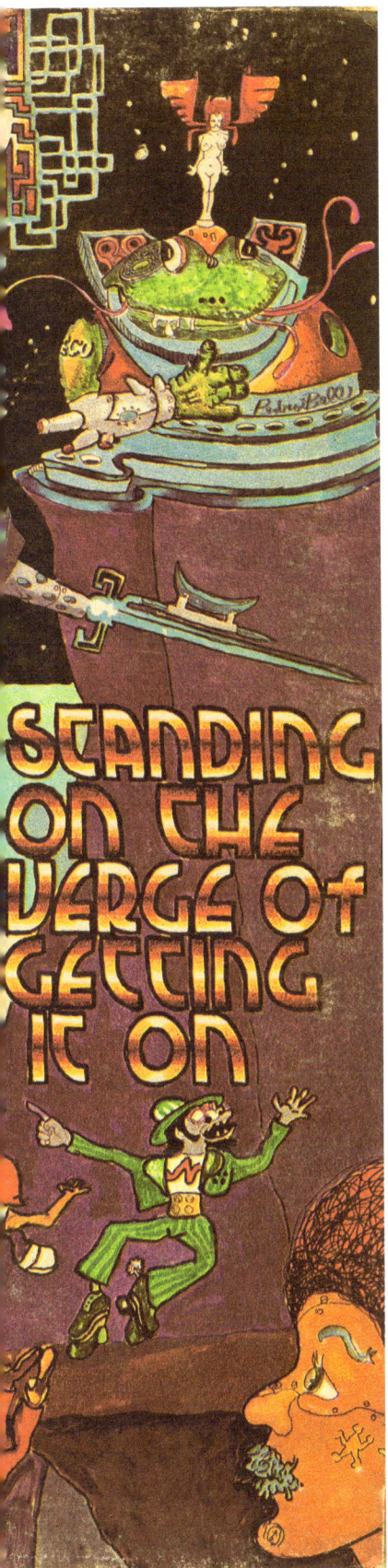

horror movies, sci-fi, spaceships, and all that.

What year were you born?

Nineteen fifty, and by the late '50s, I started getting into cars. I'm talking about custom cars, show cars, drag racing. And that got me into Big Daddy Roth and *Rat Fink*. By the early '60s, I was subscribing to *Car Craft* magazine, which would always have a full-page ad of Big Daddy Roth shirts and stuff. And, at some particular point, he employed Robert Williams to do these illustrated stories and landscapes and things around the T-shirts. And I thought, "Oh man, these are cold." That's why I was drawing monster car stuff by the mid- to late '60s.

So when the hippies started coming in the '60s, where were you?

Bradley University—that's in Peoria, Illinois, downstate. Lost my mind; I discovered the opposite sex. I lost my virginity to a closet nymphomaniac, which means I started in an advanced course. That was cool. I also got into reefer. Right across the hall from my dorm room was a Hawaiian dude. So I started relatively high on the evolutionary chain with weed. I had to come back to the ghetto after Bradley. I said, "Man, this is what they smoke in the ghetto? I can't smoke this shit!" And I got into LSD and the hallucinogens a bit, but that was a disappointment, 'cause it was a re-run, and this is why: I was actually the runt of the family, size- and weightwise. As a result, I caught every disease coming up as a kid. Ever since I was four or five years old, I remember being sick, and back in those days, docs still made house calls. Well, I didn't like getting shots because I basically had hallucinogenic trips when I did. I found out when I was fifteen or sixteen—and I broke out in hives after I had one of these episodes—that I was allergic to penicillin. And, you know, that penicillin mold is like the same shit they make the LSD from! Now, at four years old, how are you going to explain to your people that the reason why you are hollering and crying and stuff and cringing in corners is because this hallucinogenic effect has created all these overlaid images that have nothing to do with reality, but, from your mind's eye, you cannot see the difference. You understand what I am saying? So it was scary to me. Every time I got a penicillin shot, you know, I would get the trip. So like I say, in the Age of Aquarius, the LSD and the mushroom stuff, it was like no big deal to me.

What music were you listening to at Bradley?

I was checking out this group called the Fugs first. Actually, that was when I was still in high school. The WLLS superstation in Chicago had them on. They actually were the first ones to come out with an FM channel playing all the crazy stuff. And Frank Zappa and the Mothers of Invention was the next step from that, 'cause I had *Freak Out!*, which came out in ['66]. See, I was like the original "Captain Crossover." When I was coming up, my mom was like, "You are going to go to a decent school, with some kind of White population, because they're more likely to have some decent books and the PTA will take care of the business." Which did happen. And it's a sick situation, because Chicago, like most northern cities, had a school system that was ninety percent segregated. But I got a taste of grade school education with books that were up to date and all that, and I made sure everything stayed up to date. But still, I was from the projects, so I was taking advantage of the whole culture thing, because I was one of the few who would listen to both sides of the radio: Black and White. And in the '60s, that meant I heard a lot of Motown, but also, like, Frank Zappa and Hendrix and Blue Cheer and Iron Butterfly, which was the shit I was really into.

Were you still at Bradley when you first heard Funkadelic on the radio?

No, because Funkadelic came in '70, so I was back in Chicago taking art classes at Roosevelt University listening to all the White acid rock on FM. Now one day the DJ breaks out the Funkadelic record. She starts playing the intro to "Mommy, What's a Funkadelic?" and when she hears "If you suck…," all we hear is that needle scratching across the record where she pushed it! And she come on saying, "I think we'll go to a commercial while I investigate this product further." But she did come back with it, and right away, I knew that this was

the shit. Because this was everything I had been leading up to, but instead of being on the White side, this was on the Black side. And I was like, "Holy shit!" So right away, I bought that record and started trying to send letters to George Clinton in my famous illustrated envelopes.

Your "famous illustrated envelopes"?

I started doing that back in the '60s. Mom got me sent to a camp for the privileged, so to speak, out in Denton, Michigan. I went there on a disadvantaged-kid-type pass. That was the first time I was out for an extended period of time to a location where it wasn't relatives or something like that, and so I sent a few envelopes home and drew a few colors on them, doodling basically on the envelope. Now my mom said, "When you send a letter to somebody, don't be making any mistakes," or "correct your mistakes," and "use double-space letters," and all that kind of stuff. I said, "That will take a long time." You know, I wasn't really much of a typist anyway. So I decided that I was going to violate the business-letter format and put some colors on the envelope. And when I did that, I got such a favorable response, I started contacting companies requesting low-profile things like a catalog that they might charge a dollar or two dollars for or something like that. And they'd send it to me free. Well, this is nice.

And so I just started working it up. I was doing different designs, doing decent lettering. For extended stuff like a comic book, I don't have the kind of stroke for that. But the envelopes just took off by themselves, and I would get responses. That's how I ended up in Zappa's crowd. First, I heard back from his secretary or his wife, and then, when I got on to sending the second envelope, I was hearing from him directly. I tried to contact the Hendrix camp, but the only thing I had for them was Warner Brothers, and that was a waste of time. One thing that surprised me was Sun Ra. I had a P.O. box, Saturn Research, here in Chicago. I sent letters to him, asking if I could interview him, and eventually I did. I illustrated the envelopes with my Rapidograph pen and brush and markers. The Rapidograph is a drafting pen. In high school, I took basic drafting and machine drawing and basic architecture, and from that I learned about the Rapidograph pen.

What images did you put on those envelopes?

I was inspired by Big Daddy Roth and Robert Williams, so I did a thing that I call "organic lettering." When I wrote to George Clinton, that's how I did the name "Parliafunkadelicment Thang" on the front. And just standard-issue border stuff. Everything else was just geometric shapes and colors, so the organic lettering stood out as the most important.

How did you get in touch with George?

Westbound put me in contact with this dude named Ron Scribner who was doing band management in Canada, and then he went ahead and told George about me. So I kept sending them envelopes, and eventually the band got back to me. My first project for P-Funk was as a plugger—you know, a promotion artist and as a press-kit writer. See, they didn't really get out into the real world until like '72. For the first couple of albums, they were almost like a local band playing the chitlin circuit around Detroit. Canada, too, 'cause Canada was right across the road.

How did you decide what *Cosmic Slop* was going to look like and what you were going to write on the cover?

Well, guess what? I had never done an album cover in my life, so the first thing I was trying to do was to figure out how to scale that bad boy for production. I had to really guess—you know, feel my way through it. George really didn't have too much of a conversation for me on that one, except to tell me, "Do that stuff that you did on all those envelopes. The more out, the better." And when I was in mid-progress, that's when him and Bernie and Eddie came to check it out. "See what this fool's got." I had the maggot head on top already done and the inside panels, and they were cool with that. So there really wasn't much of a dialogue on that. There was some more conversation on the second one, which was *Standing on the Verge of Getting It On*. But over time, George gave me less and less direction, so I started taking risks with the covers. He started doing more albums overall, so he was getting busy and didn't always have time to send me tapes or acetates of the music, and then it got to a point where he wouldn't send me shit. And I'd say, "At least send me the damn titles, whatever titles you got." But he would always give me some input. For instance, he said on *One Nation Under a Groove*, he wanted "R&B" on the front somewhere, and he wanted song titles put on the album some kind of way. On *Hardcore Jollies*, the only thing he said on that one was he wanted "U.S. Funk Mob" to be on the front somewhere.

But you know, I don't think that we really needed to communicate much about the covers and the liner notes, because I shared a lot of my ideas with George and we was on the same wavelength. For example, when he was doing *The Electric Spanking of War Babies*, he called me up and said, "I need you to come to Detroit for this one. This is deep." So I go to Detroit and he starts telling me about the things that happened after WWII, especially after Hiroshima when the powers-that-be said, "Well, we can't be blowing up the real estate. We got to start doing some things to get the population under control without burning up the real estate. People are expendable but the real estate ain't." So George started going through the thing, and I said, "Yeah, I'm cool. I'm onto all that," which was true, because I had read so much military history and sci-fi when I was younger, and later I was reading *Popular Science* every month, which was all about futuristic concepts. And George said, "Oh shit, I thought this was going to be a hell of a thing to put together for you conceptwise." I said, "Hey, I got it covered."

Now you can see the liner notes on the record sleeve basically are the extent of his basic concept of how using media pimping to brainwash people; it all came down to the age of electric spanking. But you know, I could communicate with George like that because I was always giving him tear sheets from articles I wrote at Roosevelt University or mainstream magazines and whatnot about concepts like cloning. And I consider myself George's first sci-fi mentor on sci-fi concepts and soon-to-be-real concepts. And on all kinds of out shit like UFOs and the pyramids, or the apocalypse and other ideas from the book of Revelation. On a lot of that shit, I think of myself as source number one for George. Now with something like *The Clones of Dr. Funkenstein*, which was originally a Funkadelic concept, you could see how George made it more clever and more mainstream and could really turn people onto the shit. But he had got that information from me in '72 or somewhere in there, and that was true about a lot of the ideas in the P-Funk songs and in the cover art and liner notes.

Do you think your P-Funk work is culturally significant?

Well, when I was coming, there wasn't really any famous Black comic artists. I was aware of the vacuum and wanted to fill in the gap a little bit, because there wasn't really any Black subculture around. People like Big Daddy Roth, Robert Williams, and Robert Crumb, who were doing the shit I admired, were all White. So being able to contribute my art and my liner notes to the P-Funk music, you know, the real funkadelia, was a big deal for me, because I felt like we were putting out on the Black side what everybody thought was only coming out on the White side.

And I'll tell you something: P-Funk gave me their fan club to run—P-Funk and Bootsy's fan club. I just got overrun by the mail! In fact, I had to throw some of it out. I couldn't even keep it all. I had this tart who said she wanted to read some letters. Well, she started reading; she started crying and shit. This is why: even though this is the twentieth century—this might sound real pitiful—but I'm just telling you how the vibe was in 197x, alright? There were people who was writing stuff like, "I live in Okaloosa, Louisiana, and they don't try and teach nothing about Black history where we live. The only thing we learn over here is picking cotton and slavery, and then y'all came out and you talk about spaceships flown by Black people, and talking the Egyptians were really from Africa and was a supercivilization of people of color." Man, these people were truly outdone by knowing that this was even possible! And that was because there was nothing out there for three hundred and something years. And these people, you know, fans, kids, was blown away even at the concept. And then way after the fact, in the '80s, people would write to me or talk to me, [and] say, "Man, I been trying to find you for years. I just want to tell you this: I got such and such album, I looked at that and read it, and I didn't understand that shit. But, you know, after some changes in life, I got more mature, and I was cleaning some bud on some Funkadelic album, and I was reading that stuff again, and I said, 'Man, that stuff makes sense—these here liner notes. How did you figure that shit out?'" And, you know, you hear that shit and you say, "Damn, we was really part of something!"

Was the funk mob Black liberation heroes of a sort?

No, man, it was timing. It was timing. The baby-boomer generation. P-Funk was big for the same reason the Beatles was and the British Invasion was; [as well as] the upsurge in jazz and all that. All that happened at the same time because there was just more youngbloods worldwide in that general age category, see what I'm saying? That was a serious population bulge and when you've got that many young bloods coming up, two things gonna happen. There's gonna be a cultural revolution or another war. And we got both! And, also in the late '60s, the liberal Whites started saying, "Well, integration's not a bad idea." And Black America was saying, "We're not going to be colored or Negroes anymore; we are going to be Black people and wearing dashikis and Afros and all that." The hippie days increased that thinking a lot and gave a real merger of different cultures. That never really happened before in American history. And there were your ingredients for a cultural explosion, because it was the times that dictated that. And we was in the right place at the right time. And we freed their minds and they asses followed! ◐

One of the UK's largest suppliers of quality new and used

**SOUL • JAZZ • RAP
DANCE • FUNK • REGGAE**

www.crazybeat.co.uk

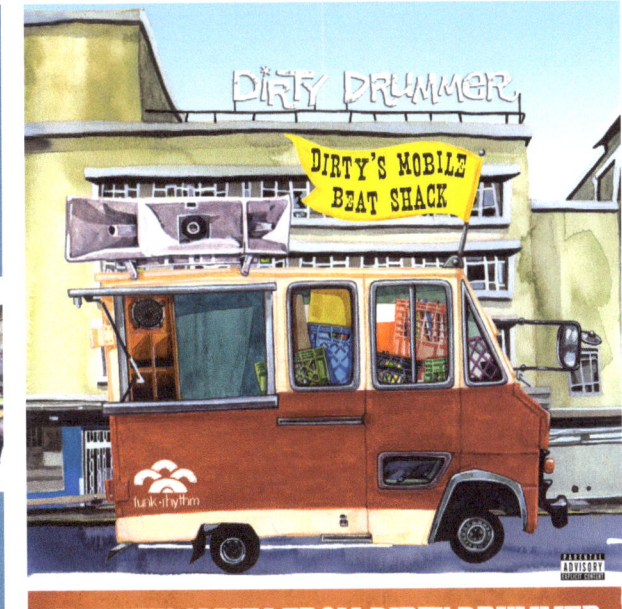

THE NEW ALBUM FROM DIRTY DRUMMER

A Big Buttery Melting Pot of Hip Hop, Funk, Soul, Jazz, Downtempo, & Afro Beat

Dirty D weaves an impressive array of beats and sounds into an eclectic mix of songs and still pulls off the unified feel that a true album should. This is an album that's definitely worth more than just a single listen. - AMPS 11 MAGAZINE

For more info check out dirtydrummer.com

OUT NOW! order online at:  iTunes music store   TOWER.COM    funk·rhythm

THE CINCINNATI CONNECTION

THE LOCAL ROOTS OF BOOTSY COLLINS AND KASH WADDY

by Dante Carfagna

James Brown's arrival at King Records in Cincinnati, Ohio, was a watershed for many young musicians in the city. It is well documented how Mr. Brown recruited the evergreen Collins brothers and their camp to assume the J.B.'s moniker upon a break with the bunch formerly occupying that role. As Bootsy and Phelps grew unhappy with the Hardest Working routine, they prowled the Cincinnati scene and assembled the House Guests, an influential band that spawned several lesser-known outfits that were populated by a cadre of talented artists, some of which also figure into the oncoming P-Funk puzzle. Presented here is a brief primer into the House Guests family and its subsequent soul branches.

THE HOUSE GUESTS

At the epicenter of this pivotal Ohio funk act were Bootsy and Phelps Collins, naturally. The brother's first band, the Pacemakers (reportedly changed from the original name, the Pacesetters), was formed in 1968 and sadly went unrecorded, yet some of the players from this combo would become the nucleus of the future House Guests family. Seeking to carve out their own niche in the music world after their departure from the James Brown roster in 1971, the brothers recruited trumpeter and J.B.'s bandmate Clayton "Chicken" Gunnels, saxophonist Ralph "Randy" Wallace, trumpeter Ronnie Greenway, drummers Tiger Martin and Frank "Kash" Waddy, and singer Rufus Allen to round out what would be a most motley ensemble. Sticking to the independent model proven by King and J.B., the House Guests founded their own label with the help of mysterious producer Walter Whisenhunt, and, in addition to their own tunes, released single records by Gloria Taylor and Ben Starr. Vocalist Taylor was Whisenhunt's main charge and probable wife, as his name is on most of her recorded output for Whizenglo, Glo-Whiz, Selector Sound, King Soul, Mercury, Columbia, and Silver Fox. Singer Ben Starr remains a little-known figure, and his release on the House Guests imprint was likely an outside production originating in Toledo, Ohio. Both "What So Never the Dance" and "My Mind Set Me Free" are impossibly funky and utterly unique recordings, showcasing a religious adherence to the One, while stretching out into realms only hinted at on the Cincinnati-infused James Brown recordings of 1969–1971. A typical House Guests show was one of wild, randy proportions, forcing the band to add "Rated X" to their name, a move not uncommon amongst working show bands in the early '70s. The group's untamed sartorial sense (when clothed at all) would mesh well with the look employed by the Parliament-Funkadelic camp up in Detroit, which the Collins brothers would depart for sometime in 1972.

Never the type to keep their creative fire from diminishing, Bootsy and Phelps would continue to record on their own even while contracted to George Clinton's sprawling acid-soul empire. The boys assumed the Complete Strangers handle during this stage of the game, issuing a raw workout called "Fun in Your Thang" for the murky Philmore Sound concern, and often performing in masks to conceal their identity and prevent the possible wrath of Mr. Clinton. Joining the Complete Strangers on live occasions at this juncture were guitarist Steve Tucker (later of the fabulous Pure Essence) and Wesley "Virgil" Maxey, who also played in many obscure Cincinnati combos, namely the Famosas and the Round Trip Tickets. As Bootsy and Phelps's focus shifted to Parliament and Bootsy's solo career full-time in the mid-'70s, the two would issue one further local 45, again on the Philmore Sound imprint. "Together in Heaven" was credited to "Bootsy Phelps and Gary," as drummer and P-Funk staple Gary "Mudbone" Cooper aided in a killer early version of what would later appear as "Together" on Parliament's *Chocolate City* album. While often simply cited as a stopgap or footnote to Bootzilla's rise to galactic bass giant, the sound of the House Guests remains crucial to understanding the early '70s Midwest funk scene and its undeniable future role in the success of Parliament and later Funkadelic works.

TOP: The 400 Years of What performing at Columbo's in Los Angeles. Photo courtesy of Gordon Hickland.
ABOVE: The House Guests circa 1971. Photos courtesy of Rufus Allen.

Recordings:
House Guest Rated X "What So Never the Dance/ Pt. 2" (House Guests 28205/ 6) 1971
The House Guess "What So Never the Dance/ Pt. 2" (House Guess 109318) 1971
The House Guests "My Mind Set Me Free/ Pt. 2" (House Guests 28821/ 2) 1972
Bootsy Phelps & the Complete Strangers "Fun in Your Thang/ Pt. 2" (Philmore Sound 30135/ 6) 1972
Bootsy Phelps & the Complete Strangers "Fun in Your Thang/ Pt. 2" (General American GAR-321)
Bootsy Phelps and Gary "Together in Heaven/ Pt. 2" (Philmore Sound 740536) 1974

400 YEARS OF WHAT

The 400 Years of What became *the* party band in the Cincinnati area after the House Guests dissolved around 1972. Led by bassist Gordon Hickland, draftees from the House Guests included saxophonist Ralph "Randy" Wallace and trumpeter Ronnie Greenway. With the addition of keyboardist Greg "Tuffy" Jackson, guitar slingers Big Jimmy Callery and Clarence Miller, and drummer Little Jimmy Roberts, the core of the crew was established. For the band's mid-'70s airing on Shad O'Shea's Counterpart label, the traps were manned by Frank "Kash" Waddy, destined to be a key player in the triumph of the Parliament sprawl and especially Bootsy's solo works. An early incarna-

tion of this outfit backed Gloria Taylor on the singer's rare single for the House Guests label, with her "Brother Less than a Man" being a primitive, rough version of the band's later release as "Do What You Like."

Recordings:
Gloria Taylor "Brother Less than a Man/ Blue Glass Bubbles" (House Guests 101)
400 Years of What "Get Down People/ Do What You Like" (Counterpart C-3790)

D.A.B. EXPRESS

The Dark and Beautiful Express were created by House Guest alumni Rufus Allen, Ralph "Randy" Wallace, and Ronnie Greenway sometime in the mid- to late '70s. Adding drummer Cornelius Roberts, bassist Donald Anderson, and guitarist Slim "Lance" Boyd, the group only managed one record in their ten-year career. The short-lived Cha-Ru-Wa label was formed by Rufus Allen, his cousin Charles Allen (a onetime member of the Ohio Players), and Mike Watson, who also doubled as MC for the outfit's concert occasions. A popular live attraction in the early '80s, the Express demonstrated the same tight musicianship seen in the House Guests, an obvious testament to their rich pedigree.

Recordings:
"Ain't That a D.A.B. Shame/ Funky Rufe-Top" (Cha-Ru-Wa 8042-31) 1978 ●

Special thanks to Chris Burgan, Rufus Allen, and Gordon Hickland. And thanks to David Castillo.

Courtesy of Rufus Allen.

"..one of the most ambitious and best free jazz outings of recent years."
Dan McClenaghan
All About Jazz

".. a who's who of downtown's finest out/jazz cats."
Bruce Gallanter
The Downtown Music Gallery

"Pulitzer Prize material... triumphant...astonishing.."
Jochem van Dijk
All About Jazz

"...a landmark recording.. compelling.. intelligent and exciting.."
Russ Musto

DOM MINASI
THE VAMPIRE'S REVENGE
CDM1006
CDM RECORDS
www.domminasi.com
©2006 CDM Records Distributed by North Country Label contact: Jim Eigo jazzpromo@earthlink.net

AMMONCONTACT
WITH VOICES

This new album from Carlos Nino and Fabian Ammon includes collaborations with Dwight Trible, Yusef Lateef, Cut Chemist, Daedelus, Prince Po, Kamau Daaood and many more.

www.ninjatune.net

Best known as the vocalist with the Pharoah Sanders Quartet and the director for the Horace Tapscott Pan Afrikan Peoples Arkestra, Dwight Trible's Living Water is re-released following the success of 2005's Love Is The Answer, a collaboration between Trible and Ammoncontact.

DWIGHT TRIBLE
LIVING WATER

TRAP MUSIC
DRUMMER FRANKIE "KASH" WADDY STAYS ON THE ONE

by Matt Rogers

"**Entropy. The measured amount of chaos.**" These are the words used by Frankie "Kash" Waddy, longtime drummer within the P-Funk Empire, to describe the most notoriously entropic band on the planet (or any other for that matter). "Controlled chaos." He should know. Over the last four decades, he's kept time for this glorious, shape-shifting mess full of Brides, Rubber Bands, Horny Horns, All-Stars, and always a few House Guests. And all in the name of the One. But for this Cincinnati native, there was a vast musical life before George Clinton. A life in lockstep with his childhood mates—the Collins brothers, Bootsy and Catfish—that took him to the mighty man who birthed that One theory and, just almost, took him on a trip with a different band of Gypsys (led by some other guy named James).

How'd you get on drums in the first place?

I started playing drums when I was two years old. It was a freaky thing. All of a sudden, Santa had to bring me some drums. It wasn't a thing where my parents enforced it. It was the other way around: I pulled them in. I'd get a toy set of drums every Christmas and get other stuff that kids get, but I'd tear up that stuff out of boredom. The drums—if you were anywhere near them—I'd freak out, not let anyone touch them. My parents were blown away. I would keep them intact for the year. And I kept going through that until middle school when I got my first real set of drums: a piece-together makeshift thing.

Were there other musicians in the family?

Not immediate family but I had cousins who were forced into it. But I stayed with it, and it evolved into me getting a real set and my first course in school, which had an excellent program. I learned to read after two weeks; music theory just made sense. I advanced so quickly until I was the youngest lead drummer in my school's history. I was so *intense* and passionate. It was something that was just in me, man.

How did you hook up with Bootsy?

I grew up playing music with Bootsy Collins from childhood. We went through so many transitions together—me, Bootsy, and his brother Catfish! See, prior to playing with James Brown, we called ourselves the Pacemakers, and we always had some type of affiliation with James. He was so huge and connected back then, and Cincinnati was a hub for him: King Records; his own management, recording studio, label, pressing plant, and manufacturing. And he had nine radio stations.

He had the whole nine indeed!

That will never happen again! He'd put out a single every two weeks, ship them to his stations, they'd break the record, then out to the nation's radio stations they'd go. So he'd keep a fresh single on the radio. He was one of the first artists to have an album with his picture on it, one of the first artists to have an equipment endorsement; this company Vox, they supplied him with everything. Bootsy and I, we'd go to King recording studio after school, as opposed to playing basketball or something, and hang out and get on those folks' nerves! Finally, they let us do something like start recording something.

We were, like, sixteen, seventeen, and everyone we recorded with, we didn't know much about: Bill Doggett, Arthur Prysock, kind of like jazz heavyweights who were trying to crossover. And then there was Hank Ballard and the Midnighters, Bobby Byrd, Vickie Anderson, Marva Whitney. We'd go out and do dates with all these people and then record with them.

So you'd be playing live and in the studio.

Exactly. See, James was preppin' us just in case. We were naïve to it all. Every local place had a James Brown wannabe. If you played live, you played his music, 'cause everyone loved it. And he'd come and sit in with us a couple of times. So, we were the Pacemakers and we would travel. We always got a beat-up car for the road; the reason being that we couldn't afford much. We knew if the car broke down, we could leave it on the side of the road and it wouldn't hurt us. We'd go out with a U-Haul truck and a beat-up car. Equipment would be in the truck with a two-man crew, and we'd be flossin' in the car like we're big-time. And it would never fail on the way back home that the car would break down! So we'd park it on the side of the highway and climb in the back of the truck, but always made sure it was late at night so nobody would see us comin' in. Then the next day we'd be walkin' around with big cheeses—smiles—flossin' like nothing happened.

What years were the Pacemakers?

End of the '60s. So we would go out and do dates with Hank Ballard and the Midnighters, Bill Doggett, and these folks from King Records. We had a Dodge Dart station wagon we could put all our equipment in and all of us—that's how skinny we were. First time we went to New York to do a gig with Hank—don't forget, he was a huge artist; Hank Ballard was the one who broke James Brown, the one who wrote "The Twist"; Chubby Checker was famous for it, but Hank Ballard wrote it—we got to the mouth of the Holland Tunnel and our brakes gave out! We went through the tunnel with no brakes. The way we stopped that car coming out of the tunnel was we had to curb the car: that's how we entered New York City the very first time.

Those were the days.

Oh yeah. One day we played this place in Cincy called the Wine Bar. I'll never forget it was on a street called Rockdale Ave. And we got fifteen bucks total. The cat told us it was a benefit and that's how he justified it. We grinned and bore it like we did everything else and kept movin'. The next day, Bobby Byrd came by and rounded us up, put us in a limousine for the first time ever, and shot us up to the airport. I mean, c'mon, man! We drove by the airport all the time and never even had looked at it—no reason to—it wasn't even in our vernacular. It took me years to realize my very first flight was on a Learjet!

So it was your entire band?

It was me, Bootsy, Catfish, Clayton Gunnells (we called him "Chicken") on trumpet—he passed away two months ago—Robert McCullough on sax. We go to Columbus, Georgia, landed, then were rushed to the National Guard Armory. Backstage in the dressing room were all our idols: Maceo, Fred Wesley, Richard "Kush" Griffith, Pee Wee Ellis. To our left was James's dressing room; he was in there. Now at the same time, we're getting yanked to the stage. We don't really have time to put it all together, plus it wasn't discussed on the way. Biggest crowd we'd ever seen in one place—sold out. Stage was so big, it was scary. We were bunched up, 'cause we couldn't even envision being spread out; it looked ridiculous. And then here comes James. He pops off songs and the keys of songs, like, "'Black and Proud,' F-sharp!" Bang—we hit. Then the next song—bang—we hit. We did the whole show like that, and it was successful. So after the show, we went to James's dressing room, and James is there saying, "Boy, y'all killed me, y'all did the *thang* I'm telling ya. I think I'm gonna give y'all $225!" And we're like, wow! We start writing these figures down. Then he says, "Nah, maybe 275." And, see, Jab'O was the only one in the JB orchestra that stayed back, and we're gauging what James is saying by looking at Jab'O, and he's being overdramatic. Every time James'd pop a figure, Jab'O would say, "Oh man, wow!" Then James'd say, "No, I'll give y'all $300," and we'd look at Jab'O and his eyes'd get all big, so we're thinking it's cool. Anyway, we wound up making 400-something dollars a week, and James said, "What that stuff you writin' over there?" "Well, Mr. Brown, we have to break it down to see what everyone'll make." And he says, "Nah, nah, that's what *each one* of y'all get!" [*laughs*] So now we're making $400 a week, got three brand new sets of uniforms with matching shoes, a Golden Eagle bus, and a truck full of brand new equipment. Needless to say, we pinched ourselves for a couple of months. It was a hell of a learning experience: priceless. But at the same time, we were just a bit too young for him. It was a bit like hanging out with your dad like he was your bud. It's cool, but at a certain point you want to be with your real buds. He was more like a father figure to us. We would laugh at him a lot, 'cause he was *corny* to us. And 'cause we were crazy.

What were some of the things he'd do?

Well, I'll tell you one thing he did which was funny as hell. He had his way of fining the guys in the band that he'd incorporated into his act. He'd be dancing and he'd open and close his hand—5, 10, 15, 20, 40, 60—whatever the amount. Well, he did it to Catfish one night. I don't know if Catfish did anything, or if James was just testin' him to see if his stuff was workin'. So he fined Catfish—poppin' this number off with his hand—looked back at us and we were *crackin' up*! We were dyin'. James was just *funny* to us. That was the end of the fine thing with us. He knew it was a new day now. See with the other guys, he'd keep them depressed, sad, and distraught. But he couldn't budge us that way. We was too fuckin' happy, young, and crazy. Plus we was fucked up. One night we played Dallas, Texas; I'll never forget. We used to open up the show with an instrumental. This night, we went so far out, so over the edge, we blacked out. James tried to stop us. We had gone a little overtime, and he wanted to start the show but he couldn't. We couldn't even see him we had gone so far into ourselves, and when we came out of it, the trumpet player was inside my bass drum. I ran to the edge of the stage, ran back. James was standing in the wings shakin' his head.

What was it like with two drummers on stage?

It was the greatest thing. Between Jab'O and Clyde, their styling was so different, I kind of got a merger of the two. When James first heard me play, he would say, "Too much foot, too much foot!" I'm thinking, "Too much foot?" Growin' up, that's all I heard on his records: guys diggin' in with the foot! But he was getting older. See, his body reacts so naturally to rhythm, and if you put too much up under him it works him too hard, so he'd want to lighten it up. I thought he was messin' with my head! On "Try Me," he'd do this little dance thing on the horn break [*imitates horns*], and one night his body contorted in a particular way and I said, "Ouch." Some of those crazy moves was a response to how the rhythm affected him. He taught us the One theory, which we brought over to George [Clinton]. The One is a frame of reference. It's where you start and come back from. Continuous cycle. When we started with James, we just jammed, we played our asses off, but the punctuation he needed wasn't there. He'd say, "Where's your One at? You ain't got no One; you gotta have a One!" And although he wasn't the most educated cat, he was highly intelligent. He'd say things his way that might've not been theoretically correct, but he could make it make sense. So from him, we understood the theory of having a point of reference to keep order in our music. We use it to this day. See, with Maceo and the other guys, he had a big horn band. With us, he had a strong rhythm section: smaller unit but a much stronger, funkier rhythm section.

Did you record with him?

Yeah, *Sex Machine* live. "The Grunt"—that's a big song. Some other stuff. Jab'O was on most of the recordings, because Jab'O showed his dedication when most of the guys had quit. Plus, James wanted to show he had some control over our situation too. Another interesting story is while we were with James, Jimi Hendrix wanted us to be his band.

You're kidding me.

See, Faye Pridgett was Jimi's girl. She had *carte blanche* in the industry. She was welcome on anyone's tour. Not to perform, but because everyone loved her. She was fun and kind of took us to another level of awareness musically, and kind of kept her eye on us for James, as far as he was concerned anyway; her function was like being our den mother. James would give her money, but she wasn't his girl; she was Jimi's girl. Faye actually took me to Jimi's one night in Cherry Hill, New Jersey. To make a long story short, she said, "Jimi wants you all in his band. But you gotta quit James, then Jimi'll pick you right up." So the guys were interested, but they didn't want to take the gamble. I was game. Jimi was playing our style of stuff that we loved. While we was with James we were listening to Howlin' Wolf, Jimi, and Buddy. Jimi wanted a more Black act. Well, before we knew it, there was Buddy Miles and those guys, the Band of Gypsys. That would've been us. I don't know how history would've evolved, if [Jimi would] still be alive or if he'd be crazy as hell.

[But] I left James [anyway], and, shortly after, the guys [Catfish and Bootsy] came home [to Cincinnati] with tails between their legs. We got back into our thing again—which we never really left—and formed the House Guests.

How much did you record as the House Guests?

Two or three songs. We didn't have a budget. And then to just sit for hours to try and convince radio stations to play our music in Cincy. But we took chances leaving the city to try and drum up some business. After James and his regimented thing, as the House Guests we went left and freed up. We never wanted to dress alike again. So we started hearing from people, "Man, y'all remind us of Funkadelic!" So we went to Central State University in Ohio one night with Gladys Night and ironically Funkadelic was doing the show too. But they had left by the time we got there. We performed and people were sayin', "Hey, y'all blow Funkadelic away!" And we're like, "Who's this Funkadelic?" So we went to Detroit and played in this place called the Scene.

Bootsy's Rubber Band's horn section, the Horny Horns: (left to right) Fred Wesley, Richard "Kush" Griffith, Maceo Parker, and Rick Gardner.

They had an upstairs lounge where you could look through these bubbles through the floor and see what was happening downstairs. We became a regular feature there, and this girl Mallia Franklin, who had seen us before, went and told George. He finally came and checked us out, and the rest is history. We became Funkadelic that night. He was looking for something new. He'd never used horns before, but when he heard and saw how horns could be used in that type of thing, he said, "Okay, let's do that."

What did you think of George when you first met?

Oh, he was cool. This is the correlation I wanted to give you. Where we didn't go with Jimi [Hendrix], ironically, we ended up with George. Same thing. What he did, as opposed to James, is he legitimized us going *nuts*. Which is probably what Jimi would've done. It was meant to happen, obviously. So we went from James to George's free-form, spaced-out, psychedelic thing. And what we did was we neutralized both worlds. We brought to George professional discipline (although we were crazy as hell and out there). I've always looked at it as a blessing. What we would've gotten from Jimi—c'mon, man—from James Brown to Funkadelic, what more could you ask for?

Bernie Worrell said he was relieved to have you guys arrive.

We brought dynamics. See, they were just groovin'; like Eddie [Hazel] or Billy [Nelson] would just start a groove and groove all night. We were playing arrangements, breakdowns, hits, and at the same time we were all funky. One thing about George that has always impressed me is that he'll be open to doing something new. George is like, "Yeah, okay, on the One, that's how it works? Okay, cool. Oh, y'all go crazy too, okay." We taught him that One theory and he still uses it till this day.

You didn't have Jimi Hendrix but Eddie Hazel wasn't a bad alternative.

Jimi loved Eddie because he could play his ass off. Something else that blew him away was vocalists. Jimi said the only reason he took a chance on singin' was because of Dylan. But his guitar, I don't know where he got all that. Bass, rhythm, lead all into one. He took something from everyone he played with, like Little Richard, the Isley Brothers. Then Eddie took from Jimi and what he learned from the church. Eddie Hazel was a hell of a vocalist.

So you first appear on *America Eats Its Young*, then the P-Funk enterprise just takes off. What was that like?

For me, it was crazy, because I just stayed on the road. One time for four years straight, no break. 'Cause when Bootsy's Rubber Band was on hiatus, I'd go out with Parliament-Funkadelic. And then when we formulated the Brides [of Funkenstein], I was the original drummer. They were like an alternative to P-Funk. They got into the White places, the alternative clubs, and got the television gigs because they were classy and funky and 'cause we got them from Sly Stone. Lynn Mabry and Dawn Silva. It took us to another level as an organization. The band was actually the Rubber Band without Bootsy and his brother.

Talk about the funk festivals.

You know what the funk festival thing was? We were the only Black organization to ever compete with the Kool Jazz Festival. That was very risky, because they had their dibs on everyone. They were the big dogs in the game. We competed with them as a movement. I think the first one was the Isley Brothers, Chaka Khan, Rick James, Bohannon, Rubber Band, and P-Funk. The Isley Brothers thought they should headline. We said, "Okay, no problem." So we went on before them, and, as we were performing, they were walking out. That's not a put-down; it's just that they didn't know. And to show you how things work, we did a show with Kanye West about two years ago when he was starting to get big in the game. His ass wanted to headline an outside thing in Montgomery, Alabama. He was respectful when he met us, but to the promoters he insisted being the headline. We said, "You don't really want to do that." And after he performed he came to us and apologized: "I don't know what I was thinking; there is no way in the world I will ever try to go [after] you guys again."

Was there much rivalry back in the day?

We never really fed into that. We made spoofs and jokes on records and stuff, but we never really fell into that on a personal level. We actually tried to get cats to work *with* us. Everybody opened for us. Especially for the Rubber Band: Cameo, ConFunkShun, Ray Parker Jr., Brass Construction. What really blew me away was the guys that came after us fought like cats and fucking dogs! Zapp Band, Rick James, Prince, Morris Day and the Time—they were really going at it, man! The only thing we really tried to do is get Earth, Wind and Fire to work with us, and they never would. It wasn't because we were nasty to them or anything; they just didn't want to deal with it. We played the Spectrum in Philly one night, revolving stage and everything, with the Commodores when they were starting to blow up. Lionel Richie came into the dressing room and said, "Kash, we ain't working with y'all no more. We ain't got to. Shit, we ain't working that hard no more!"

Ohio Players?

One thing about the Ohio Players that hurt them is they overproduced their projects. They couldn't reproduce them onstage; it was totally different than what you heard on the radio. We had a totally different approach. A lot of people don't realize the thought and theory that went into making our records. We went through a period where we didn't listen to the radio or look at TV, 'cause we wanted it all to come from within. Our theory was do great recordings but make them so you can do them even better live. If we couldn't reproduce it on stage, we knew it would be a failure. One thing about a fan is they're watching you very close, if you're lucky enough to have a fan base.

How has your fan base changed?

We got such a funny group of fans. All breeds. We got one fan that will go through all kinds of hell to get backstage and then stand in the dressing room the whole show. Not even peek out just to catch one song. Like listening to the radio, just standing there—won't even move out of our way! [*laughs*] When we first started doing the marathon show, I'd be playing four hours a night, no break. And as we got older, we started playing longer and harder! I'd look into the audience and I actually felt sorry—people were, like, proppin' each other up. And after a tour of that, word got out and then people started preppin'. I started seeing some of the same faces in different places, standing there for four hours straight! We also got fans that will time the show and just catch the last two hours. Sometimes promoters are so worried about us getting on the damn stage; our problem is getting *off* the stage. We are notorious for getting the plug pulled on us.

How many shows would you say you've done?

Ah man, don't do that, don't do that! When we [the House Guests] first became Funkadelic, we were an underground act. Funk was a bad word, for real! We had a cult following. We couldn't even say the word *funk* on radio or TV, or put it on posters for public display. I wish we had a lot of footage on that, 'cause those shows were crazy. And the irony is, that's when we had an all-White fan base. Then when funk became a household word, *then* they shipped us as a Black act! Now this is gonna weird you out. When we started gettin' those hit records, all of a sudden the distributors would call us, bitchin': "Hey what you guys doin'? We need product!" So we contacted the label, saying, "What's goin' on? These cats are goin' off 'cause they don't have product. They're sold out and we kept getting brushed off." One guy finally told us the truth, and said, "Hey man, these guys don't want you to leap over to suburbia, they just want you to do well in *urbana*." And that blew us away. First of all, that was the furthest thing from our understanding of how the game worked. As far as we were concerned, we were hot, happening, pressing a bunch of records. They were actually controlling our destiny to that degree. They wanted us to wear suits, wear the uniform of what is a so-called successful uniform for America or whatever. They wouldn't play us in suburbia.

Too much chocolate for the vanilla.

Everything we did would have gone triple platinum. This was before and after *Chocolate City*. They were controlling our distribution. That's why so many people in suburbia hadn't heard of us. Maybe back in the day [there were] a few cocky ones that had enough nerve to come over in urban America and run back and tell everyone about the Mothership. And it spread. Everyone wants to see the Mothership who hadn't seen it. So now they can't stop suburbia, and now, that's a big part of our audience. So it went from all White to all Black to a majority White now. It's crazy. [*laughs*] And we're the most sampled group of all time. The DNA for hip-hop. See, funk to me is a way of life. It's a lifestyle. Not just a fad or fashion or something cool to do. What you hear on those records, we were living them, believing in them, and that's why they stand to this day. ●

Visit Kash Waddy at frankiekashwaddy.com.

GREGORIO HOWE Y COMPADRES
SALSA BLANCO
LATIN SOUL FLAVORINGS

PRODUCED IN THE MISSION
SAN FRANCISCO, CALIFORNIA
PRODUCTO AUTENTICO DE MISSION

NET WT 10 TRKS.

FEATURING:
GREGORY HOWE
CALVIN KEYS
DANILLO PAIZ
NATHALIE SANCHEZ
RAY MARTINEZ
MATT MONTGOMERY
THOMAS MCCREE
MIKE RINTA
MATT CUNITZ
DOUG ROWEN
AND MANY MORE.

www.widehive.com

WIDE HIVE RECORDS

ON GROCERY SHELVES THIS SUMMER

TIMMION RECORDS

Building...BIG!
Nicole Willis & The Soul Investigators
"FEELING FREE"
Timmion # 013 - 7" Vinyl

OUT IN SEPTEMBER!
DIDIER'S SOUND SPECTRUM
Long Awaited re-issue LP
in Stores in September
By Lifesaver RECORDS
www.lifesaver.net

Still Going...Strong!
Nicole Willis & The Soul Investigators
"Keep Reachin' Up" LP/CD

Timmion Records are now Distributed in the USA by
LIGHT IN THE ATTIC RECORDS and DISTRIBUTION www.lightintheattic.net
www.timmion.com

Mackrosoft Presents:

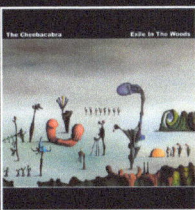
The Cheebacabra: Exile In The Woods

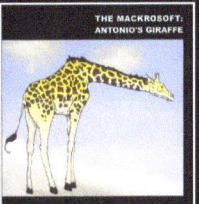
The Mackrosoft: Antonio's Giraffe

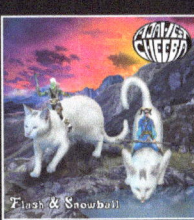
Aja West & Cheeba: Flash & Snowball

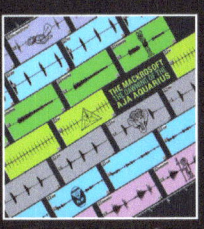
The Mackrosoft: Aja Aquarius

"The Mackrosoft crew have thus far sailed under the funk radar, but their mythic notoriety will soon become ubiquitous."
-Wax Poetics

www.mackrosoft.com

FROM THE CRIB TO THE COLISEUM

STRETCHIN' OUT WITH BASS LEGEND WILLIAM "BOOTSY" COLLINS

by Thomas Sayers Ellis • photos © Michael Ochs Archives.com

FEBRUARY, 22, 2006 — THE ROCK AND ROLL HALL OF FAME

For the sake of history, let's start at the beginning.

Well, my mom, she grew us up. No dad. No dad in the house, but I always felt responsible for the things that went on in the household. And Mama always had a belt, too! And she would wear us out. I never got a male perspective of that, so I was always out in the streets. Looking up to the males in the streets that did certain things I dug, like entertaining—the players on the streets—the hustling. But then I got interested in music, because I wanted to be like my brother, "Catfish" [Phelphs]. He was playing guitar. I really got interested in music, and I think that's what started it.

During the *Player of the Year* tour, a pre-concert cartoon told the story of a paper boy who was transformed into a superhero. Throughout your work, the lyrics and the licks seem to be referencing a silly seriousness. Growing up, did you watch a lot of cartoons?

Oh yeah, I loved them. That was the thing coming up. When we went to school, we'd have the subject book—English, whatever it was—that would be the book the teacher would see. Then you'd have your comic book inside of that book, ya know? The teacher would say, "Did you hear me, William?" "Oh yeah, I got it. I got it." And at the same time, I'd be reading *Spider-Man* or *Batman*. We was just in to the comic thang, and I guess it just spilled over into the music. We just wanted to have fun with it—music. And since we looked like cartoons anyway, we just ran with it.

How did you end up at King Studios?

Oh, that was a blessing! Well, actually, a guy in Cincinnati was an A&R guy. His name was Charles Spurling and he would go out and look for new talent, new people to come in and record. So he came out to a club one night. We always played benefits.

We never got paid and weren't looking to get paid. At that time, we was just looking to have fun and have a good time. That's pretty much what it was all about. So he came out and saw us playing and said, "Yeah, I want y'all to come over to King's and be my recording band." We was like, "Yeah, King's. Ain't that where James Brown is?" He said yeah. Our whole thing was, okay, if we get over in King's, we'll get to meet James Brown, Hank Ballard, the Isley Brothers. We were cocky kids off the street, and, like, "Yeah, we bad!" And we really believed that. We got over there and lot of the different producers that was producing top acts at that time wanted us to perform on their records. Once we started doing that, word start getting around. Then Mr. Brown heard about us. He didn't want to be left out. It was like, "Who are these young dudes over here making all this noise. Making all these records?" And it was like, "Yeah, that's Bootsy and them." He said at some point, "I'd like to meet them, send them out on the road with Hank Ballard and Marva Whitney." And, actually, that was our first professional gig.

Where were you when James Brown's band walked out on him? Do you remember the night in 1969 when that phone call came?

I'll tell you exactly where we were. We were on Gilbert Avenue at the Wine Bar playing a benefit for the door, and I think it was just us and the bartender. And we was just as loud as I don't know what. And everywhere we played, we just played loud, whether we had one person in the audience or a thousand people. It didn't matter, ya know? Then all of the sudden, the phone rang. The bartender came up to me and says, "Hey, Bobby Byrd wants to talk to ya. He wants to talk to you about playing with James Brown. We had took a little break. We was like, "Yeah right, Bobby Byrd want to talk to us about James Brown." So we kind of laughed it off, and he was like, "Nah, he's on the phone." So, I went and answered the phone and sure enough, it was Bobby Byrd. And he says, "How would you like to play for James Brown?" And we're like, "You're joking. You must be joking." And actually, we had kind of made friends with Bobby Byrd, because he was the only one we could get to

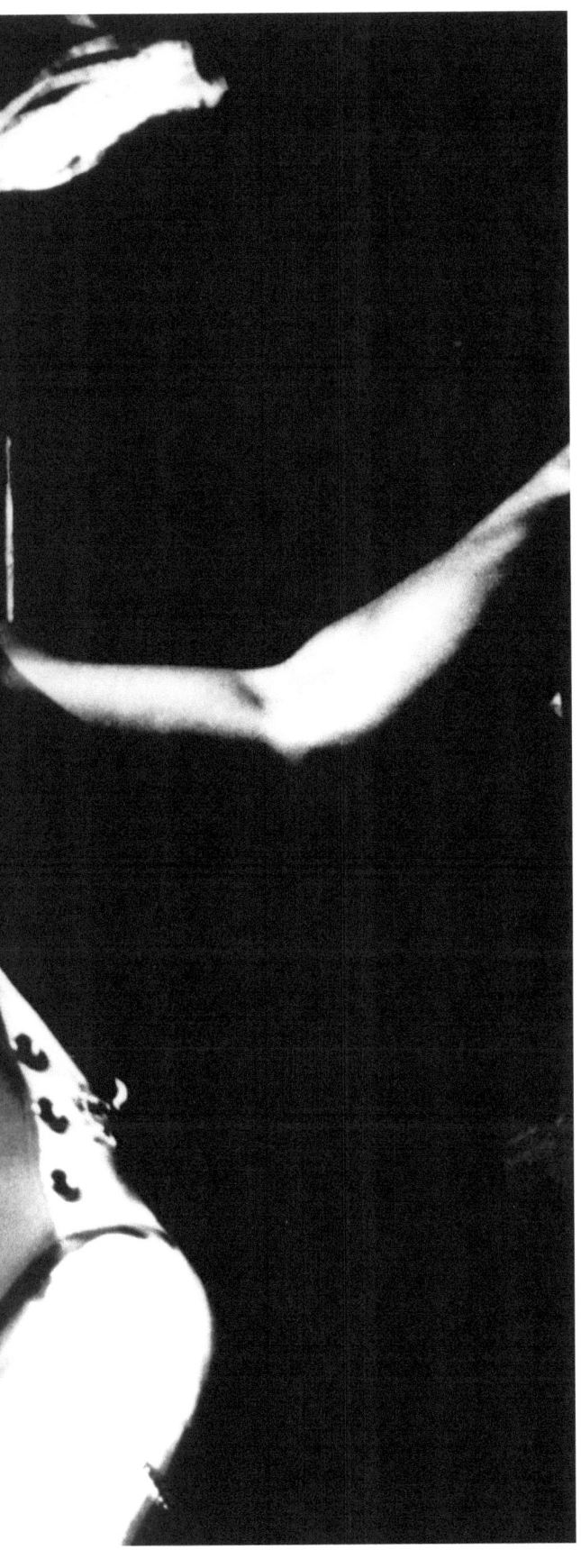

back then. He really befriended us and brought us in before we even got with James. So, yeah, he was like, "James really want y'all to be the band. Actually, I'm going to fly y'all up." We was like, "No, no way. James's jet! No way." So we had never flown in a plane before. So we was like, "Okay, we'll be ready. We'll be right here when you get here. See ya when ya get here—yeah right." And he actually flew up there within about forty-five minutes. He was there at the club: "Come on, we got to go now." So we had on our tie-dyed jeans, my Afro was leaning to the right. And we were wearing them little round eyeglasses from back in the day. Just cool. I said, "Well, can't we go get cleaned up? We don't want to go like this." He said, "No, we gotta go right now. James is waiting on stage." We said okay. Next thing you know, we was on an airplane, my Afro was in the back of my head and we was flying up forty thousand feet in a Learjet. And I had never been on a plane before. I'm seventeen years old, flying on the Godfather of Soul's plane and I'm like, what is going on? Talk about a kid trippin'. I didn't know what was going on. So when we get to Columbus, Georgia—I never will forget the look on the people's faces when we got there. We came through the back door. I already had my bass out, ready to throw down. And as we were walking in, people started hollering, "You're late!" We didn't know what that was about! They asked us, "Y'all James Brown's band, ain't y'all?" We didn't know we were James Brown's band yet! So Bobby Byrd says, "Let me take you back here so you can talk to the Godfather." So we get back there in James Brown's office—I got to get y'all in James Brown mode. I'm going into his voice now. He says, "Look here, Bootsy, y'all some bad boys. But y'all playin' with the Godfather tonight. So when I drop my arm down like this here [*Bootsy motions*], I'm gonna call out the songs to you. Y'all ready?" We looked at each other and said, "Yeah, Mr. Brown, we're ready."

But y'all knew the songs already?

Oh yeah, inside and out. And he knew we knew them. So we hit the stage and sure enough, he calls out a song, drops his hand down, and we were on it! I mean, we were onstage with the Godfather of Soul! Man we were going to wear that mutha out! We thought we were wearing it out. We hit every move. We knew all of his moves. If you noticed, it wasn't so much about his singing and screaming, it was all about his body. His moves. You had to pay attention! I ain't never paid attention that much! I mean, every little move he made, if it was with his foot, you had to be on it. Wasn't no getting high, I'm sorry! If you were high on that set, you wouldn't have made it. Done. So that's the straightest time I've ever been onstage! And that's the truth!

So what did you learn from him? Jab'O said that your style of bass playing had the most movement he'd ever heard. But Brown had to focus you on "the One."

He was the one who brought that to my attention. Because I thought I was doing something different. It was like, I don't want to be like other bass players, just holding the foundation down. I wanted to play a lot of things. "Son, listen to me now. I'm the Godfather of Soul." He always had to lecture me, and it was cool because, like I said, I didn't

have a daddy back home, so I guess he felt like he had to fill those shoes. And he was like my dad. "Son, you got to stop doing all them things and just give me the One." So when I started doing that, he started to like it and I could tell. So I figured, if I could give him this One and play all them other things…I think he'll like me. So I started giving him that One that he needed, and playing what I felt. See, a lot of people at King liked that we played what we felt. In fact, James's string arranger asked me and my brother if we could read music. And we said, "Oh, yeah, we got this!" So he counts it off and says, "Okay, play what's in your face." And so we said, "Just count it off and let us hear a little bit of it before we start. We want to make sure we're on point here." So they count it off and the rest of the band played. And then we said, "Okay, count it off again." We was on it. So after the session, the arranger called me and Catfish back in the room and says, "Everybody just loved what y'all did, but y'all can't read a lick." So we were like, "Yeah, you right." But I said, "We wanted to play with y'all so bad, and we knew we had to know how to read." And he said, "No y'all don't, because the feel y'all got—don't nobody else got a feel like that right now." He said, "Don't worry about it. I'll work with you." So that's how we got the gig of playing with the big orchestras. First, I lied, and then I came back and ate the lie, but at the same time, I gave them the something that they wanted.

But you did eventually leave. How did that happen?

Well, really, the reason I left was because of the older people that had been there—because I was the one who could get his way with Mr. Brown. Yeah, I was the young one. They'd say, "Let Bootsy do it!" You know, like that old commercial [for Life cereal] used to say, "Let's get Mikey to do it! He'll do anything!" "Let Bootsy do it! He'll do anything." So they kind of used that with me, with James. Like, "Tell Bootsy to tell Mr. Brown that we need so and so. That we need this." And I'm saying to myself, "I don't need nothin'. I'm just groovin'!" And it's like, "Okay. If y'all want me to go in there and do that, I'll just go in there and tell him and see what he says. And every time I would go in there, he'd do it, ya know. But this last time, they said, "We need a raise! You know, he should be paying our hotels and he should be doin' this that and the other. Bootsy, you need to go in there and tell him!" I'm like, "Okay. I'll tell him. All he can say is no." So I say, "Okay, cool." So I go in there, "Mr. Brown, everybody's feeling like they need some more money, you know." He said, "Now, Bootsy, let me tell you somethin', son. Now I know they puttin' you up to this." In other words, he knew I didn't have sense enough to go in there and do that! Which I didn't, 'cause I wasn't thinkin' about nothin' like that. You know, all I was doin' was havin' fun with the girls, watchin' the artists get off; it was just a great time in my life.

You traveled to Nigeria with James Brown's band. Talk about meeting Fela Kuti.

Africa, man—we got off the plane and they started bowing down to us: "Yeah, James Brown's band!" And I didn't really know how to take that other than, "Yeah, we James Brown's band, but I didn't feel worthy of the praise they were giving us, because I was just this knucklehead, long-haired sucker from off the street, and all of a sudden, I'm with James Brown's band, and then I got a bunch of people praising me. We go to the hotel, and we find out that Fela Ransome [Kuti] has invited us to his club. And he was like James Brown over in Africa, so we went. And, man, I told them to take all those praises back, because they were the ones that needed to be praised. 'Cause them mugs was so on it. They had some grooves there that I had never heard or felt in my life. And I couldn't believe it. I just could not believe it. I mean, you could be ten miles away and you could hear the drums. You could be carrying on a conversation and the next thing you know, your body starts movin and you can't control it! And you're like, "Damn, what's wrong with me? I know I ain't high!" So it was a whole other experience. And speaking of high—can I go there?

You got to.

We're in the car. It's me, Bobby Byrd, Vickie Anderson, Catfish, Clyde, and an African driver. And just so you know, they didn't have policemen, they had army men policing the place. And they did not play. For instance, this one guy came to the show. He was blind, couldn't see nothing, but he busts into the dressing room, run up the steps, yelling, "I want to see James Brown!" And then the army guys just fell out, laughing. And we were like, "What are they laughin' at?" The cat is blind, and they laughing, saying, "You wanna see James Brown? He can't even see!" And that really killed me. And then they clubbed him all the way back down the steps. So when I saw that, I thought these cats couldn't give a dang about me if they did that to him. So what I was thinking while we was riding in this car, and I got some dirty stuff on me, right? We're riding and all of a sudden we see the army men coming up. And I start getting a little nervous because we're in the car gettin' a little tipsy. And the Army guys are coming towards the car, and I'm like, "Uh oh." We got to put this stuff away. We got to roll the windows down and get this stuff out of the car. All of this is going on in split seconds. Dude comes up to the car and right before he gets there, I say, "Vickie, put this in your purse. They won't look in your purse." She said, "No, I'm not taking that stuff." She says, "Put it in your boot." So I put it down in my boot, right? So dude comes up to the car and says, "Okay. What's in the boot?"

Damn!

And I did exactly what you just did. I could not believe he saw that. I was saying to myself, "How did he know I had put that stuff in my boot?" So he kept talking and the guy was trying to explain to him. I don't know what they were saying. The two men were speaking an African language. So the army guy says, "Okay, but I want to see what's in the boot!" So, okay, I'm getting ready to give in now, because I know I'm busted. I start to go down to my boot and the driver gets out and walks to the back of the car…to the trunk. The *boot* is the trunk! Ah man. I mean, my heart was in my boot! So he goes back and checks the trunk and says, "Okay, you're good to go." I looked at Vicki and Bobby Byrd, and I was through! My high was gone. I said, "Here, y'all can have this stuff. Just take it!" I mean, it was the bomb too. That stuff over there was the bomb! And I just gave it away. I quit getting high for two days.

Do you think you changed the direction of the James Brown thang?

That's what people say. I think I brought what I did to the music. But I can't say that I changed James Brown's music. I can only say I was so glad to get an opportunity to be there. I mean, whatever happened, just as long as I was there and learned what I learned. I can't take credit for that. All I can say is that, that was probably one of the best times of my life. Clyde and Jab'O—I had some of my heroes behind me. I mean, they were just like heroes for real. Even when I got there and was able to really get to know them, they were still heroes. It's like, say you're with a chick; you think she's this way or that way, and you get to know her, and you say, "It's not exactly how I thought." But you know I can't say that about the James Brown experience. It was everything that I thought and more. So I would hope that I brought something to it because that was a great time.

Let's jump to Detroit circa 1971. Y'all thought you had your own style until Mallia Franklin says that you guys have the same vibe as Funkadelic and that you should meet George. Do you remember meeting George for the first time?

Yeah, I definitely remember that. Wow. Mallia had come down to this club called the Love Club. It was a place where all of the youth would get together; you know, the young bands would go on stage and kind of compete for the gig. And that's what we did a lot. That's where "Let's Take It to the Stage" came from. Competing and taking each other's gigs. So Mallia heard us, and the other bands heard us too, and they were like, "I don't know who these mugs are, but we're not going on before them and we're not going on after them." So the reputation started going around, and George started hearing about us. And the Mallia says, "You need to go talk to George, because y'all got so much in common. I think his band is gettin' ready to leave him. They're having all kind of problems over there. Not enough drugs, whatever. They have had it up to here with George." So she takes us over the next day. I remember walking in the house—I'm kind of semi-trippin' too. Walk in, and George didn't have no furniture; got about three rooms. When you look straight through the house, you could see all the rooms. No furniture in none of them. And he sittin' in the last room, in the corner, got his legs in like a Buddha thing—you know, with his head down. He got a star on one side and a moon on the other shaved in his head and the rest was bald. He got a sheet on. His feet—you know he got these big *"Boy, I say, Boy"* feet. You know who I'm talking about: Foghorn Leghorn! Actually, I nicknamed him that. Yeah, but y'all ain't heard that from me! But he had these big feet stickin' out from under his thing. And I'm like, "Dang, this is gonna be fun." So I walk in and started talkin' and next thing I know, we just started clicking. It was like, "We'll go out with you, but I gotta make sure I keep my band's name. The band name is the House Guests. But let me back up a li'l bit. Before that even happened, the Spinners had called us up to come to Detroit to play behind them.

Go back even further to Philippe Wynne.

Philippe was from Cincinnati and he was our lead singer in our first band, the Pacemakers. So when we got to Detroit, we go as the House Guests featuring Philippe. But when we get there, we said, "Okay, the Spinners done called us, so we going to have to play behind them."

You were going to have to play "Rubber Band Man" instead of "Stretchin' Out (In a Rubber Band)."

Yeah, and after coming from James, after being in a band wanting to do our own thing, we want to come on stage and act a fool. We don't want to be cool with suits on. We don't want to have our shoes shined. We want our 'fros over here, leaning. We don't want to get fined! If we get with the Spinners, it's going be the same crap! So we say, "If that's the only choice we have, then we'll play with the Spinners. So when we get to Detroit, and Mallia tells us about George, we're like, "Oh yeah, that would be the bomb. Funkadelic instead of the Spinners? I wanted to tie that in so y'all know that. So we go over there and we talk to George and he says, "What are you going do with Philippe?" I was like, "Well, he could go with the Spinners." I mean, they needed a lead singer too. They wanted all of us. They wanted the band and the lead singer. Philippe would have a star spot with the Spinners, and we would have a star spot with Funkadelic. Because then, we could get up there and act a fool like we wanted to. So it all worked out. It was kind of like written already. I mean, it was like, *wow*, when it went down like that. I talked to Philippe about a year later, and he was like, "Man, I'm so glad y'all did it like that." And it was almost like he thought that I thought of that. [I told him,] "Nah, it just happened like that."

The first Funkadelics got turned out. Did you guys get turned out?

That's why my hat goes off to George so much, so regularly, because everybody wanted to hang with George on the stuff—drugs—and I ain't met nobody yet who can hang with George—not James, not Sly, not [Little] Richard. No one. None of them could hang with George! But everybody in Funkadelic was like, "I'm a Funkadelic, man." You know, being a Funkadelic, you had to be one of the wildest, craziest mugs in the world. Brothers just didn't do the things that we did.

I heard George got blowjobs on stage and used to use the bathroom onstage.

I'll tell you a small story. George was known for always making the gig. Never late, even if nobody showed up. I remember one time: me, Catfish, and George showed up to a sold-out, outside gig. We were the only ones that showed up. George said, "Well, we gotta go on. We're here." We went up, killed them for three hours. No drummer or anything. Just a guitar, a bass, and George singing. Killed them! The crowd loved it. Then again, they were all blitzed out of their minds. George was never late. He was always on time. He also showed me how to promote myself. We would be at radio stations back when funk was a bad word, and they would be like, "We can't have y'all talking about funk." George would say, "Well, motherfunk y'all then." And the more he said that, the more we got interviews to talk about the funk. But it just goes to show his persistence—'cause people were like, "We want the funk. We don't care what y'all critics say." And that's where [the lyric] "we want the funk" came from. George didn't make that up. The people came up with that. George heard it and said, "Yeah, let's take that. Come on, Bootsy, let's go to the studio." We would give the people what they gave us.

You were about to discuss the outrageousness.

We had a gig in D.C., at Howard University, and everybody is like, "Where is George?" The gig started at eight o'clock and it's a quarter till. The rest of the band is getting frantic, because no one knows where George is. It's like, how high can you get before showtime? You know what I'm saying, because they're doing angel dust, and all that craziness. But then I thought, "I know where George is." Everybody's like, "Go find him, Bootsy, go find him." So I start going to all the different bathrooms at the school, and I look up under the stall and I see these chicken feet. Back in

love" and challenge kids to use their imaginations. I wouldn't be like, "I want to F you." It was fun to take that kind of slang—street terms—and do something different with them. George and I had a constructive competition to see who could come up with the best one. It made it fun, and it really opened my lyric thing up. It gave me depth. Everything wasn't in your face. Actually, when we were doing "Be My Beach," I was in the studio, joking with George with that voice. I was doing it as a joke, and he said, "Yeah, I want you to put that on the record." And that's what George was real good at, and still is—good at hearing things and saying, "Yeah, that's different. Let's do that." And even now I pick up stuff that I hear or even stuff I do—I make sure I put it down. I got my little tape recorder. When I was with James, a lot of things flew in and I never got a chance to put them down, but with George we had the availability to go into the studio all the time. With James you didn't have that. You had to keep it in your head, until

FUNK WAS A BAD WORD. BUT THE PEOPLE WERE LIKE, "WE WANT THE FUNK. WE DON'T CARE WHAT Y'ALL CRITICS SAY." AND THAT'S WHERE THE LYRIC "WE WANT THE FUNK" CAME FROM. GEORGE DIDN'T MAKE THAT UP. THE PEOPLE CAME UP WITH THAT.

the day, George was known for wearing these big ol' chicken feet on stage. They were really big and had three toes! He use to wear these things, and I saw them sticking out from under the stall! I said, "George!" He didn't say nothing. I was like, "I know that's you, man. Ain't nobody else going to have them feet on but you!" So, he ain't got no rap, right? I hear moans. I know what's up. So I say, "Okay, I'm going give you a few more minutes, but we got to hit it, man. We're supposed to be on the set." No rap. So I stand outside the bathroom, and a few minutes later he come out and I say, "Man, we gotta get on the set. Let's go, let's go." But I later learned what was happening. Two chicks had him in there, and they were wearing that mother out. Yeah, they was wearing him out bad. George don't miss no show. He ain't late. So y'all know he was getting wore out. And when he finally come out, we killed them. Yeah, that was a great show.

On the song "Be My Beach," your signature voice and persona come out for the first time, as well as your talent for punning silly double meanings.

With Bootsy's Rubber Band, I tried to attract a younger audience than Funkadelic had. I would take words like "funk" and expressions like "I got the munchies for your

you could get somewhere where you could put it down and that was hard, man. You're like, "What was I thinking five minutes ago? That was the bomb! You should have heard it, man!" "Yeah, well why didn't you record it fool?"

You gave up the funk, a lot of funk, in order to get a record deal and your own band. What made George keep his promise to you?

Well, I think, you know, it's because I did everything I said I was going to do. No matter how loaded we got at night, no matter how crazy the girls got, I was there at nine o'clock in the morning before the engineer was there, ready to roll. I was right there, and he saw the dedication that no matter what—I mean, all the rest of them cats were drugged out. I mean, I was too, but I had to get up. If you wasn't at the studio first, you may not have [gotten a chance to record]…because it was a hundred of us. And if you didn't get in there, your song was shot. I was like, "I'm gon' have as many songs as I can get. I'm a get up. Yeah, I'm gonna party as hard as y'all, but I'm gonna beat yo' ass to the studio tomorrow." And I did that.

Was that the James Brown discipline?

Yeah. That was the discipline. I learned that from James.

Being on it. James had a saying. He'd say, "Bootsy, let me tell you something, son. If you ain't on heel and toe, you got to blow." And me and Cat used to look at each other: "What the hell is he talkin' about?" And after we left him, we figured it out. If you ain't on heel and toe, you got to blow. He meant you had to be on it, on everything. On top of it. And when we got with George, I kind of lost that for a minute. I lost it on purpose because I wanted to have fun. You know, when you on it like that, you can't really have that kind of fun. You got to be responsible. I didn't want to be responsible, man. I just wanted to play music for people, have a good time. I don't owe nobody, don't nobody owe me, we just havin' fun. That's the way musicians looked at it back then. Let's just go have a good time, I ain't gotta pay nobody, and everything is cool.

"Bootzilla." That's a monster moment. That was your first number-one single—in 1978. It's also a hell of an ego leap.

Yeah, from the crib to the coliseum. George actually pushed me. You know, once I developed the character, it was like, "Oh no. You ain't stopping now." I was cool with Bootsy. Bootsy get out there with his little star glasses on and did his thing. I wasn't like, trippin'. It was just a good time. But George was like, "Nah man, you got to be the rock star now. You got to be the Black rock star." And it was like, Bootzilla was going be the one to take me there. So I found somebody—the dude that made my star glasses. I brought him the design I wanted for my glasses. They had to be sparkling. When I walk out on the set, it's going to be bling everywhere. I wanted to add that flash to the funk.

You've said many times that you had to find something else, because Larry Graham was already the baddest muthaplucker that ever lived. Talk about the birth of your space bass.

Oh, he was *the* muthaplucker! When I was in school, I used to draw stick men with a star guitar and star glasses. And I never knew what it was, but I spent a lot of time doing that. Pretty much all my time besides reading comic books. So when I got with P-Funk and that time came, George says, "Okay, it's time for you to go do your thing now." I was like, "For real, man? Ah man, you going to let me? Ah man!" Okay, I got to go get me some star glasses and get me a star bass. George looked at me like, "Where are you going to get all that? You ain't got no money." But I went and found these mugs. And these people had so much, and they felt sorry for me because I had enough nerve to be in there talking about all of this bigness, and ain't have a pot to piss in! I'm telling this boy how to make my bass, and didn't even have a down payment. You know: "I want it like this. It's gotta be in the shape of a star." I had everything already drawn out. "I want the pick-ups here." And he's like, "Man, this is incredible." I took it to all the boys in New York, and they were like, "Ah, get out of here. Ain't nobody going to make no money with that crap."

But it was all about finding the right person that wanted to be creative. And I found the dude in Detroit that wanted to take the risk, the risk at making this bass. His name was Larry Pless, and I got with him. He worked in an accordion music store. And I'm going show you how God works.

Check this out. I see "Accordion Music Store," and I'm saying to myself, "Ain't no way there's someone in there who knows a thing about guitars." And something just kept saying, "Go in there. Go in there and tell them about your space bass." I went in there, and the guy who owned the place says, "I don't do guitars, but I got a youngster in the back…he makes guitars." So he sent me in the back, and I started talking to this guy. And we just started hitting it off. I had to hype him up first because I didn't have any money. He was like, "Wow, this is incredible." So I sold him on the idea, how incredible it was, and he said, "Yeah, man. Let's do it." I say, "Well, just get started on it and I'll be back. But he says, "But you got to give me some kind of something to get the materials. I say, "How much you need?" "How about $150." I say, "I know I can get $150 from somebody." So I actually bummed around a little and got the $150 and brought it back to the guy. That taught me to always be a man of my word. If I say I'm going to give you $150, I'm gonna get that $150 from somewhere. I mean, I didn't go out and rob anyone. I talked to a few chicks that kind of liked me: "Baby, I'll pay it back to you next week." So they hooked me up.

How did you get Maceo Parker, Fred Wesley, and "Kush" Griffith of the Horny Horns to join the Rubber Band?

Oh, that was easy. When we were with James, I told them. I said, "Man, when I get out of here, when I leave James Brown, and I start making it, I'm going get you cats to come out with me. Would y'all be up for that?" Fred and Maceo was like, "He just talking." I say, "Nah man, I'm for real. I'm getting out of here and I'm going to get something happening." And they said, "Okay."

What happened after *Player of the Year*? There was a huge gap before *This Boot Is Made for Fonk-n* was released.

I couldn't get high off of what I was getting' high on. This ain't it. It ain't why I got out here. I got out here because of the music. And I started to see that we couldn't do anything without getting high. It was like the high came first. Getting high was first instead of the other way around. It used to be, first we'd play music, and then maybe we'd get around to getting high. Things reversed on us. For me, coming from James Brown, that was backwards. Something was wrong with this picture. It didn't feel good anymore. I found myself, instead of partying with people—and [at] all the gigs, that's all we did was party, party, party—instead, I was running from people, and trying to hide and trying to get a minute to just take a breath. Because when you start rolling like that, and everything you touch starts turning into gold, you don't get a minute to yourself. And I didn't know nothing about that. I was just acting a fool all my life, so I didn't know nothing about the responsibility of being there all the time, on call. I would wake up in the middle of the night and a mug would have a microphone to my mouth in the hotel room. And I'm wondering, "How did this mug get in my room?" So I started hiding from people, and that wasn't cool.

What is Bootsy doing now? Has the player settled down?

Yeah, in a good way. I got a beautiful wife now [Patti Willis]. She's helped me a lot with settling down, because when I was coming up, the streets taught me never to be attached to one person. I could be in a city and have four or five chicks coming to see me at the same gig. If I got down below four or five women, I was like, "Wait a minute, I got to add some more here." So I was all screwed up with that one. I had grown up with the intention of not getting married because I had seen all my friends get married, and the next thing you knew, their lives were screwed up. I got to be around forty-five years old before I started thinking about it. And guess why I start thinking about it? This is the sad thing. I started feeling like I was losing my mother. I'm saying to myself, "Okay, wow, if I lose my mother, who else is going to have my back? As far as everything that goes on here at the house while I'm out acting a fool. Somebody got to have my back."

You don't go out with P-Funk or your own band as much as you used to either.

I don't want to go out like everybody else. I want to be the one to make the choice. If I want to perform, I want to perform. If I feel like I got something to give you in a performance, then I'll give it to you. Y'all know I came up with the "If you fake the funk, you nose will grow, baby." So I can't go out there faking the funk. You know, if I ain't feeling it, I can't bring it to you. So how can I talk about it without being about it? And that's the problem now. Mugs out here talking about it, but they not being about it. People do it in the church. People are talking about it. And my whole thing is what you see today is I'm a book. Can you read me? And I wanna be a good book.

Damn, I wish I had said that!

I just feel like you can't tell anybody what to do. James used to tell me what to do: "You can't be up here getting high." And the more he told me not to, the more I wanted to do it—and the more I did it. So it's all in the way that you approach people. And I'm in search of that way. I don't know it, but I think I'm on the right path. And Snoop, all of them come to the Rehab. My studio is called Bootzilla Rehab, and we don't do the things we used to do. No. It's the Rehab. We do music. You get high on our terms. That's cool. I done did it all, probably much more than any of y'all. But it's just the fact that the young people come in, and they expect me to be getting high, they expect me to be doing this and that. And I get off by just seeing, "Oh, I know what y'all expect. But I'm gonna give you somethin' different." And that's been my whole thing. I want to give you something different. You know, now kids be talking about I'm different this and I'm different that, and they all got the same gym shoes on.

Casper, Bootsy, Bootzilla, Star Mon, the Player, Gadget Mon, Captain P Mo, Mug Push, Count Tracula, and Zillatron. Do you know who you are now?

Yeah, you want me to tell you?

Yes.

William Collins. ⚫

Thomas Sayers Ellis *is a poet from Cleveland, Ohio.*

HIT MAN

THE FUNK MOB'S GARRY SHIDER AND HIS MIGHTY BOP GUN

by Matt Rogers • photos © Michael Ochs Archives.com

"**We were basically the bad guys. The outlaws.** Not like Earth, Wind and Fire: they were the good guys," informs Garry "Diaperman" Shider, the diaper-wearin', pacifier-suckin', guitar-playin', gospel-singin', bop gun–totin' P-Funk vet. "Like how the Beatles were the good guys and the Rolling Stones were the bad guys, we took advantage of it too." Taking advantage of what might not scream "opportunity" is something the native of Plainfield, New Jersey, has clearly mastered, whether the context be the streets, church, or a pair of pants ripping just before showtime. Still a teen when first summoned to join the P-Funk posse in 1970 by the then Toronto-based George Clinton, Shider made an immediate impact, cowriting the *Maggot Brain* classic, "Hit It and Quit It." And then there's his ethereal lead hovering like a ghost atop the nasty pulse of "Cosmic Slop." Not to mention his gilded voice and guitar chops on classics he's composed or cowritten, like "One Nation Under a Groove" and "Atomic Dog"—you know, the ones that've been sampled, oh, two, three times. He wants you to remember, though, that it all started at home, many, many years ago. "I got started in music through my family. My father, grandmother, all my brothers: we all play. We sang gospel first in a Baptist church. My father played guitar, so I tried that first. Then I tried the clarinet and the drums. Eventually, I got to piano. I was too afraid to try the organ in church. The guitar stuck, though."

How was the music program at school?
Well, it was cool till they took it *out* of school. Around the fourth or fifth grade, it was gone. You might've had a glee club left, but they took all the drums, violins, and all that stuff out and that was the downfall.

So when did you crossover to secular music?
I was doing all that at the same time. I liked all kinds of music. Songs like [*sings*] "How Much is that Doggie in the Window"—Patti Page I believe that was—"Silent Night," "Hound Dog," and "Love Me Tender" by Elvis (this is when I was real young now); I was even into the Mills Brothers. And then we had all the gospel groups: Clouds of Joy, Sons of Emmanuel…

What was being played at home?
Everything, because my brother had (still has) a large record collection. He got everything you could think of that came out in the '50s, 'cause my aunt would give him records. She would get them before they came out. He's still got them in his basement: 45s, 33s, and even 78s. See, there were seven of us; I was the first. I was the nerd (if you let "Boogie" tell it).

Why were you the nerd?
'Cause I was always in the house taking care of the kids. My mother'd go to church every Monday, father worked. The babysitting part was my gig. While everybody else is hanging out, I'm in there babysitting. I had to sneak out and try to get back before anybody got home.

To hang out with George at the barbershop?
Everybody did that [who] was in Plainfield, dude! Kept you off the streets. That was the spot. Eventually, after the barbershop, we had the Neighborhood House, the King Center, the Y, the Freedom House. Community centers, basically. My first rock and roll band—me and Boogie's—was at the King Center. The director bought us a bunch of equipment, 'cause he knew we liked to play. I was thirteen maybe. It was myself, Cordell Mosson, Leroy Williams,

Brian Watkins, Michael Arendale—that was the nucleus. We was playing anything that was on the radio, dude; we was the band! Goin' around to all the correctional centers and schools to perform.

Did you take lessons?

I tried but they threw me out! They called my mother and said, "Don't send him back here," because I already knew what I wanted to do, that it was a waste of time. In fact, I had won a scholarship to the *dagnum* place: Gregory's Music School on Front Street. That was the big music store in Plainfield.

So who were the big groups in town?

You had the Admirations, you had Sammy and the Del Larks, you had the Darkside, the Bel-Aires, the Mad-Lads, the Exsaveyons (I used to play with them), Linda Jones, Kool and the Gang, Soul Dukes, Lloyd Price's band, I believe, was down there. And we also had the Ambassadors, which was [Glenn Goins's] group and his brothers.

What the hell was in the water there?

That was the thing, man. Just about everybody in Plainfield played an instrument. Played and sung. It was a musical town, for real! Especially for guitar players.

Really? Why do you think that is?

I really don't know. But I'm not mad at 'em. [*laughs*]

Was there much of a musical rivalry then?

No, no, we were all cool. We'd just take it to the stage, you know what I'm sayin'. That's how we got off: "Let's take it to the stage." Play in the park, the schools, weddings, firehouses, wherever you could plug in. At that time you could carry the gear yourself, no roadies, you were the roadie. Now, I thank God for roadies!

You kept at it, stayed focused. How did you meet Cordell Mosson, aka Boogie?

I've been knowing that little dude since we were three years old. He lived around the corner. We were babies together. All our career, we've been together. Boogie and me know each other like the back of our hands. Two peas in a pod. You always say, "Where's Boogie and Garry?" Never just one of us. He was always on bass, but at the King Center he was the drummer. We was trying to put a band together; we were taking hubcaps, radios, turning magazines around to make a microphone—we was slumming then, slumming hard. My brother—he used to sit down when the Beatles came around and just drum, drum on drums he made out of paper, practicing, saying, "Yeah, we gonna have us a group, y'all!" We had the family band at the church and we went around to other churches to perform. In fact, we were gonna make gospel records before I got into the rock and roll, got into this funk stuff. My father was finished with me. I blew the whole shot!

They weren't too happy? They didn't get it?

No, they got it. They were supportive of whatever we wanted to play, but it wasn't part of their plans. But it still worked out, look at it. My brother did some stuff with

Alicia Keys recently. We definitely have it covered now—keyboards, drums, guitar—we want to get together and do the Shider Family Band; that would be interesting.

Did you know Bernie Worrell then too?

Yeah, we all knew each other. We all grew up in Plainfield. [The Parliaments] were just older. Eddie, Billy, Bernie, George, Calvin, Fuzzy, Ray, Grady, Ernie Harris, [and] Richard and Frankie Boyce. The Boyce brothers was one of George's first guitar players. They the ones who had the Admirations that me and Boogie was in. Songs like "Moonlight," "Ain't It Funny"—doo-wop-type stuff. Frankie got killed in Vietnam; they all got drafted around the same time. We were about to be signed to Warner Brothers. It was right after "Testify" came out, right around '68. Then the Parliaments came back and got Eddie, Billy, Bernie, and Tawl Ross.

You and Boogie then had your group, U.S. (United Soul). When did you start that?

We started 'bout '68. We were playing funk. Then around '70, George came to Plainfield and sent us to Canada. Myself, Boogie, his brother Larry, "Slim" Edwards, Harvey McGhee, Reggie Turner, a dude on keys named Bill. Record labels had approached us, but they just didn't work out right. We stayed together till like '72, when we officially came on with George. In fact, "Rat Kissed the Cat" and "Broken Heart of Mine"—that's U.S. [as well as "I Miss My Baby" and "Baby I Owe You Something Good" on Funk-adelic's *Music for Your Mother* comp].

So how would you describe the evolution of Parliament-Funkadelic, musically, since you witnessed them from such an early stage and then joined as they were about to take off?

Well, they tried the doo-wop thing, and they was cool with that, but then all of a sudden they got a chance to play with them big amps and then they got turned out. [*laughs*] George would say, "Hey, wait a minute. We ain't gotta worry about keeping the suits pressed—none of that kind of shit—our hair done." They went from cool to hippies, and I mean downright hippies!

How long did that transformation take?

It didn't take long, trust me. Maybe a year of that doo-wop shit, if that, before they was takin' acid and everything else. The music just got louder and louder and louder. You couldn't hear the singers half the time anyway. With Tiki, Bernie, Eddie, Tawl, and the singers, it was at least ten up there on stage, without horns. By the time we got to the *Mothership* [*Connection*], that's when it really became a funk opera. There weren't any Black acts like that. Not what we were doing. Jimi [Hendrix] was doing rock. Ours was just purely funk. Which is gospel, R&B, blues, jazz—all of it just mixed up. Then Bernie—he'll figure out any keyboard, and go that Berklee University on your butt: Bach, Beethoven and all that kind of stuff. You never knew where he was gonna go and then where he was gonna end up. But then what I learned as we played together more and more, and I guess from growing up together, we knew exactly where the other was gonna go. Back in the day, nothing was planned; you'd just lay it out.

You came into the P-Funk fold around when Bootsy did.

They came in the group first. But I was officially in from *America Eats Its Young* on. And then Bootsy had to go on his own. We would've held him down. I think Philippe [Wynne, who would later join the Spinners] was in their group at one time. Bootsy and Catfish put everything on the One. It was a good thing. Brought some order to the chaos. [*laughs*] That's the difference in Parliament and Funkadelic. Funkadelic is loose, guitar oriented. Parliament's got horns and little fancy arrangements.

Aren't you on Parliament's *Osmium* record?

Well, I see my name on there somewhere. I was always writing. In fact, my first song was "Hit It and Quit It," but they spelled my name wrong: Garry Shila. Plus, we were doing a lot of sessions then. That's how we survived. We had four, five sessions a day! Running from one studio to another, and all these groups I'd just met—didn't even know them by name. I was all over their records for writing and producing for Westbound. Lot of Donald Austin, Dallas Hodge, Teegarden and VanWinkle, Chairmen of the Board, Fuzzy's.

Was it a lot of live recording in the studio or overdubs?

We first started out live—a lot of that. Then later on it got to overdubbing. Cordell and I would compose a lot of stuff, then bring it in.

And you were in the shadow of Motown. How was that?

It was cool. Went and did stuff over there too! It was one big musical family. Detroit was really beautiful, and I wasn't even there when shit was really jumping.

What are some of the songs you wrote or cowrote that you're most proud of?

Lot of them. "Atomic Dog." "One Nation [Under a Groove]." "Do That Stuff." "[Night of the] Thumpasorus [Peoples]." "Uncle Jam" was cool too. I create by just hanging out. I mean, I can hear it in my sleep.

"Presence of a Brain"—that's a great song; it's a whole 'nother vibe.

From the *Up for the Down Stroke* album! Thanks. That's when you could tell the sound was changing. Bootsy was playing lead bass with that Neutron pedal, which gave everything a different sound. Bootsy also overdubbed a lot of his drums, 'cause we'd play in the studio with a click box—we called it the "Man in the Box." Then Bootsy's Rubber Band took off. That was a whole 'nother live element. Mudbone [Gary Cooper] and Peanut [Robert Johnson] from Baltimore—they came together, hooked up through the Rubber Band, then eventually started singing on P-Funk stuff. Great singers. And then Bigfoot [Jerome Brailey] came and changed the beat. You could really hear the beat. Before him was Tyrone Lampkin. He was more like Billy Cobham; actually, they were kind of good friends.

And before him, Tiki—he had the funk. The fastest foot in town. He'd do a drum roll with his one foot [like] what people'd do with their hands.

What were your audiences like?

Seventy-two got kicking: mixed, Black, White. By '75, '76, it got really Black. Funk was a bad word. Ain't been that long since it got in the dictionary! Parliament was more radio, which helped the cause. It was all Black music to me. It was one big jam/funk party then. We didn't care who showed up. We'd still plug in if nobody was there! In the early '70s, before the Mothership, you have to remember, we were the opening act. We'd open for people like New Birth, Chaka Khan, Mandrill, War. We'd slowly move up the pole. You know, they'd give you twenty-five minutes, so you'd have to hit it! Now we play four hours. [*laughs*]

So then the Mothership blasted the universe.

As it became bigger we started to take on the world. We were like, "James Brown meet the funk!" Then we took his horns. The Mothership tour [in 1976]—the funk festivals were real big. The Mothership opened the door. Kicked it wide open. That's a hard act to follow too, trust me.

Were there bands still trying to follow you?

No. And then "Flash Light" was more like a disco record. But much heavier, with a different twist. We used the basic elements, then took it from there. That changed the whole stream of music when we started using synth basses. Then in '79 came the Sweat Band. I wrote a lot of their stuff. It's all just one big thing, one big blur. All of them have been good to me. Things died down a bit in the '80s, but I kept recording with George. Shit, we had "Atomic Dog" in '83. Then we worked with the Red Hot Chili Peppers—wasn't like we hadn't played with White rock groups before. We did a lot of that in Detroit with Iggy Pop, MC5, Ted Nugent, stuff like that. We're getting ready to do something now with Dave Matthews. See, I'm used to this; I grew up in this. Sure, we all get on each others' nerves. But we get our downtime. You gotta take care of yourself. You just do it. I can do it. I didn't get into it to get out of it.

Finally, I gotta ask: who first started wearing a diaper on stage?

George did first. Then one time, I tore my pants and I didn't have nothing else to wear, so then I did. You stay cool up there when it's hot, but it be cold too. I get both of them. Just remember: funk ain't goin' nowhere. Funk ain't goin' *an-y-wheeere*! ◯

BOP ART
ARTIST OVERTON LLOYD TURNED P-FUNK MYTHOLOGY INTO FINE ART

by Richard Edson and Edward Hill

AND IN A FLASH OF LIGHT, SIR NOSE GIVES UP THE FUNK.....

Did you draw when you were a kid?

What really got me started with art was: my dad was a jazz musician; he had a bass drum that had this [hand-drawn] pinup girl on it. That's my earliest memory of a drawing. I remember staring at this pinup girl—and I must have been three or four years old—and I kept waiting for her to move. Later, when I was in school, one thing that I did not know [was] that I was nearsighted. I couldn't see past the paper on my desk. But what I could do was focus on what was directly in front of me, which was usually some girl's booty that I ended up drawing on my paper instead of the math. So I can't add, but I can draw a booty. Never thought it would amount to anything though.

When did you first hear George Clinton and Funkadelic?

I remember hearing "Testify" on the radio [around 1967]. In Detroit, at that time, everything was Motown, Motown, Motown. I just remember growing up listening to all these Motown sounds, and it seemed like they were made just for me, just for my generation. We were really into the Marvelettes, the Supremes, you know; we really felt these people, probably the way the hip-hop age feels Snoop Dogg. And we didn't think anybody could outdo the Temptations. They were the kings. So when Parliament came out with "Testify," we saw it as a lame challenge. I was in junior high school, and I remember being in the lunchroom and there being a debate about "Who are these guys?" They sounded like the Temptations drunk on alcohol. We didn't know from marijuana. Some of the more radical kids would come in blasting "Testify" on a radio and kids would go bananas. By that point it was apparent that, okay, these Parliaments were here to stay. They definitely usurped the Temptations. At one point, I found myself at a concert, an outdoor concert, and I remember seeing these guys. They first came out with the suits on, and I remember hearing a Motown beat. Like, *dum dum dee dum*. Then it would break into *boom, boom, boom*, and they got real nasty. I do vividly recall somebody jumping off of the stage and seeing the audience freaking out at the front and running from this person who was probably George Clinton, you know, doing his voodoo stuff. All I knew was that something in front was scaring the daylights out of people. And then we would see Parliament popping up on a show called *The Robin Seymour Show*. It was a show out of Toronto, I think, that was shown in Detroit, and Parliament would come on this show looking crazy. I remember George had stars and moons and crazy crap cut into his head, pre-punk, and they would sit around a hookah and smoke marijuana. George confirmed to me later that it was not a prop. They had that much audacity in those days; they were smoking it on TV.

At that time, what were you doing in terms of your artwork?

I was trying to figure out, "What does it take to break into art history as an African American artist?" In '72, I did a painting of the Black Moses in oil. I think somebody who worked with Isaac Hayes saw me sketching in a cafe and somehow they got me to present Isaac Hayes with this painting [of] himself as the Black Moses. I had little women sitting around his shoulders and on his chains and things. Anyway, I remember being at his birthday party, a big line going around the block, and I was able to get in with this painting and get up to this room where Isaac was holed up, gave him the painting, and a week later I saw a picture of him in *Ebony* magazine, with the painting behind him. And that was thrilling for a kid, you understand? I didn't have a clue of how to break into the fine-art world, but I started seeing some possibilities with records. And I was into Funkadelic in part by virtue of Pedro Bell. Because, outside of the artist Corky McCoy, who did the *On the Corner* artwork for Miles Davis, Pedro Bell was the only other African American artist that I could really find out there in the medium. I [had] learned how to draw White folks pretty good, but I couldn't figure out how to draw Black folks.

The examples didn't exist.

Right, and the ones that existed were the stereotypes from the '40s with the inner-tube lips. So the only way to learn how to draw them was to draw my friends. So, when I saw Corky McCoy's work, that was like, *wow!* I got another interpretation of what we look like. Pedro Bell just took it over the top. As far as I'm concerned, Pedro Bell is one of the early pioneers of hip-hop. The bottom line is Pedro Bell presented me with something that I could relate to, [that] African Americans could relate to. And that was a first for my generation.

How did you start collaborating on comics and art with George Clinton?

Okay, I must have been in high school, because I was on a bus going to the library when I came across a club called

20 Grand. The 20 Grand was mythic in my high school, because we would hear rumors of these insane events that would happen when Funkadelic was there. But I was too young to even think about going to the 20 Grand, so I must have been sixteen or seventeen. Now I don't want to sound corny, but something actually told me to get off the bus, right then, to at least look at the 20 Grand as I was riding past. I must not have had my glasses on, because I remember seeing this fuzzy stuff in the parking lot, and I couldn't even make it out. I just noticed, like, a bunch of colors. I gathered that it must have been the band outside of the club. I remember thinking, "Well why would they wear these weird alien-looking costumes if they're not on-stage?" I think I had on me a book called *Soul Is* that I had done with a puppeteer in Detroit. So I gave them my book and some sketches, and Archie [Ivy] took my number. I figured I never would hear from them again, and I didn't. But I would see them at Coball Hall and get backstage. I would meet George every now and then and he would never remember me. Now you have to fast-forward to when I'm about eighteen or nineteen and living in New York. I didn't care about P-Funk anymore. I was into it when I was in Detroit, but when I moved from Detroit, they were over. It was at this point that I was doing caricatures in the street to survive, and I got a call from a friend of mine named Joey Zallerbach saying that the P-Funk was doing a wrap party for *Clones of Dr. Funkenstein*. Joey was an engineer with George at one point and we knew each other in Detroit. So I got to this party and someone introduced me and George, and I said, "Hey, I'm the guy that you never remember." He said, "Oh no, you look familiar." And he said, "Come sit down next to me." And he says, "So you draw?" I say, "Yeah." Then he asked me if I could draw a spaceman, so I drew a little sketch. And he asked me if I could make the spaceman a pimp. I asked how would I do it, and he said to put a cape on him. I put a cape on him.

He says put diamonds on the cape and at that point he lost me, because I was too new school to know about old school pimps and diamonds. So he's giving me pimp lessons, putting diamonds all over this space guy. It was like an instant audition. I drew the picture, he loved it, passed it around to everybody. So I'm being reintroduced to his world, and he's telling me that he's been getting colonics. He asked me if it was possible to draw an expression somewhere between pain and pleasure, and he wanted me to draw a nurse giving somebody an enema and put an expression on the guy's face right in between pain and pleasure. He was really interested in that moment between those two emotions.

But, bottom line, after this party was over and I ended up back at my place, I figured I would never hear from these guys again, because I broke every rule in the book. I gave away free artwork without a contract, without payment, without anything. I just gave it away. But I got a call from Archie Ivy saying that they loved the stuff, so I found myself traveling with them while they were doing interviews. I figured George would be just insanely drugged up and drunk and everything. But someone offered him a beer and he wouldn't even drink it because he said it's better to sound crazy and act crazy, than to be crazy for real while doing these interviews. So that took me aback. I watched him do all these interviews sounding crazy and high as hell. But he didn't indulge in anything until we got back to the hotel. Anyway, one day in the hotel I'm sitting there, and the door burst open and this guy comes through the door with a box of rubber noses. They had been looking for these rubber noses for weeks to promote Bootsy's [single] "The Pinocchio Theory" [from the album *Ahh...The Name Is Bootsy, Baby!*]. So they finally had these noses and they were so excited about it, and George started playing with the noses and putting them on and getting his woo on. And that really freaked me out, because here's this older guy acting ten years younger than me. So I decided what I wanted to do was sketch him in the act of being super childish. So I'm doing this sketch of him playing with the rubber nose and he catches me. I'm thinking he's going to throw me out. Instead he says, "Oh that's neat, put this hat on me." The next thing I know, George is trying to name the guy right there on the spot, and everybody was trying to name this guy and someone said Cyrano de Bergerac. George liked the rhythm of that and he says "Cyrano de Bergerac, Cyrano de Bergerac, Cyrano Minus the Groove." It was Tom Vickers who changed it from "Minus the Groove" to "D'Voidoffunk." So Sir Nose D'Voidoffunk—that's the name of the character. About one week later, I was in Detroit and I picked up a *Jet* magazine, and they were interviewing George and he was talking about this new album, *Funkentelechey vs. the Placebo Syndrome*, starring the old ghetto legend Sir Nose D'Voidoffunk. I was like, *wow*. And so, when I got back to New York, I found myself doing the comic for that album. Archie tells me the story of the Placebo Syndrome, explains the whole thing, you know. And, basically, between Archie and George, I got the story that it was an analogy for the kind of stuff that was going on with *Star Wars*. So it was Starchild playing the Luke Skywalker role, I guess Dr. Funkenstein was being Yoda, and of course Sir Nose was being the Darth Vader. And the only thing is, George wanted to do all of this with no words, which I thought was ridiculous, because it was the craziest story I had ever heard in my life. Plus it had something to do with placebos, which who the hell knew what that was? So I decided to just write it as cryptically as possible. See, George wanted it mysterious like a puzzle, because he thinks that Black people are supersmart and once they catch on to something, they're done with it. So he wanted to give them something that they would never quite figure out even twenty or thirty years later, and I think he's kind of achieved that.

He's like a cross between Disney and Rod Serling and Malcolm X, probably. He takes it all way-out. I always thought of myself as the guy who just made it backstage, and I was documenting for all the people who didn't make it behind the scenes: "Look, guys, look what I'm actually seeing." And I did see it as an opportunity to give some dignity to Afrocentric art. I'm one of these artists who, although it might look good to you, to me it never looks good. I'm a perfectionist. I never thought I was nailing it. So, a lot of what George gave me was the freedom to screw up. Because George wanted to see the rough sketches, you understand, the scribblings. He said the same thing with his musicians. He doesn't want to have Bernie or Black Bird or anybody have to prove that they can make music. He wants their afterthoughts. And so that gave the freedom of failure from my perspective, gave me the freedom to, like he said, do the best I can and funk it!

Looking at the reverence in which P-Funk is held by the hip-hop community, do you feel like you were successful in your contribution to Afrocentric art?

I remember hearing one of the Beatles asked, "How did you enjoy the Beatles era?" And he said, "We missed the whole thing. We were too busy working." That's kind of how I feel. I kind of missed all the contributions, because I was too busy trying to get away with it, trying to make it work, and trying to communicate, you know, and not really being sure if it happened, and feeling like I'm sort of in a vacuum, even at the peak where we got big audiences and people are going nuts. So I says, okay, this is only happening because George promotes it. He makes people believe that we're legit, you understand? But I never took personal credit for it. It wasn't until years after the thing was over—this must have been the mid-'80s or something like that—and I remember I was at Venice Beach, broke again, doing caricatures, and I see this hip-hop kid walking on the beach and he had a jacket with the *Gloryhallastoopid* character painted on the back. And I am like, "Wow, man, where did you get that jacket?" He said, "I painted it. It's copyrighted and you'd better not steal it!" That was my dream come true right there! That's when I first got that my biggest complaint was that I couldn't copy other African American artists, but I became that artist that kids thought they could copy to learn how to draw. ◐

Richard Edson *and* Edward Hill *have together interviewed Charles Wright and James Gadson for* Wax Poetics.

earmint
another early evening
FEATURING
MURS
ROC C
DIVERSE
PSALM ONE
OUT
JULY 25TH
OUT NOW:
LONGSHOT AND COPPERPOT
COPPERSHOT
ISSUES
FEATURING
KRS-ONE
DIVERSE
BRAINTAX
Copper Shot
available at:
UNDERGROUNDHIPHOP.COM
WWW.EVRECORDS.NET

You've found some gems thanks to Wax Poetics. You've made some sick tracks, recorded, mixed and even tried mastering them yourself, but they don't sound as official as other joints you've heard on the radio and other CDs.
That's when you need to get at us.
mixing & mastering
www.redsecta.com
323.574.5008
get your levels right.
Since 1997, we have been giving independent artists, labels & recording studios that professional sound. Since '97 also, we are the only ones who'll give you a completely free test master. $50 off when you mention this ad, good until 10/31/06.*
*4-track project minimum

JAZZ TRAVELS
COMPILED BY
CASBAH 73
HITOP027CD
A Global Expedition in Search of the Good Groove
CD digipack
and double LP
on sale September 4th
distributed by:
soul seduction
listen up on: www.hitoprecords.com

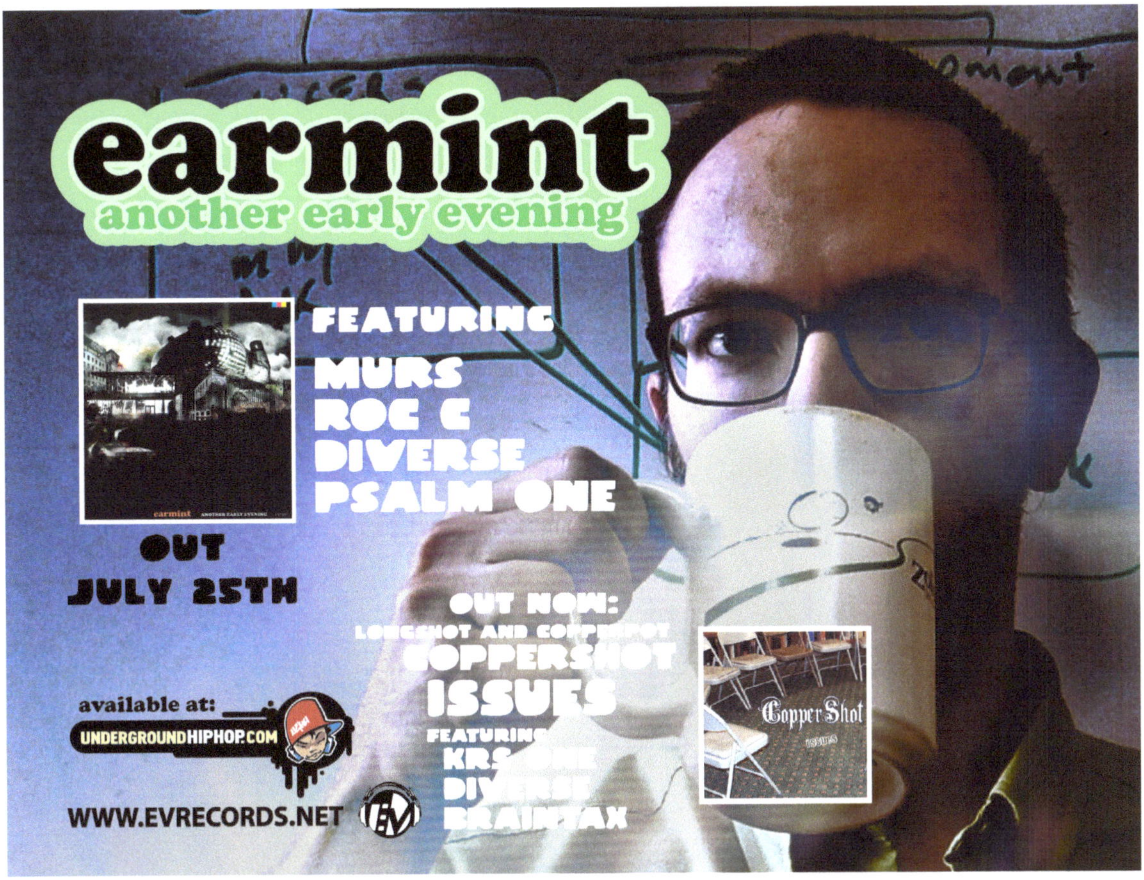

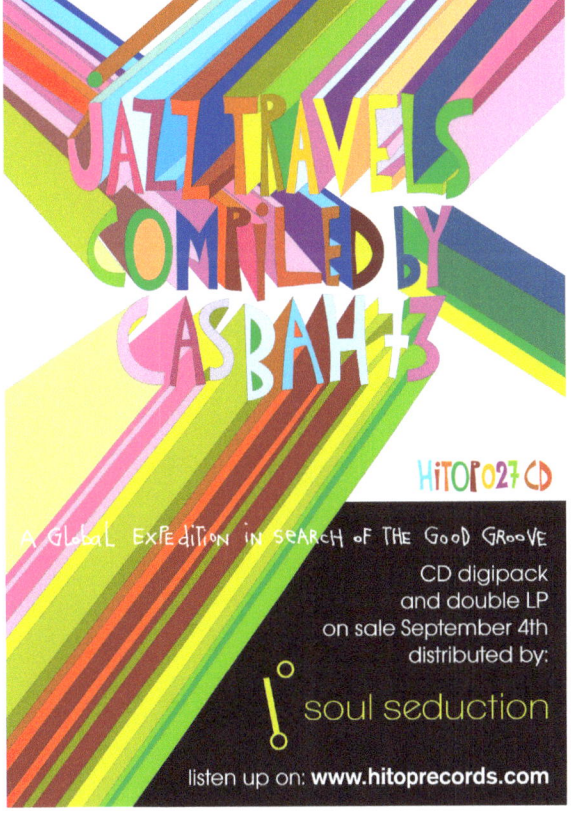

BROTHER FROM ANOTHER PLANET
THE COSMIC JAUNT OF P-FUNK LEADER GEORGE CLINTON

by Matt Rogers • photos © Michael Ochs Archives.com

Dead of winter, and a few frosty-ass miles from where old-school hippies and ghosts of the borscht belt mingle in this washed-out New York town, whose restored prewar theater boasts recent performances by America, Air Supply, and a Pink Floyd tribute band. Tonight, the P-Funk Express has decided to park their two cosmically sloppy buses here anyway and I have an appointment with the big man, Dr. Funkenstein. While waiting I rap with two little kids (dreads nascent, pushing five and six if they're lucky) "manning" the merch table. "We can't read, but these are P-Funk shirts," they say. "The band that's in there is P-Funk. We like their music 'cause our dad plays in it. We like the one where they're talking about where they go to funk." Who says there's no hope, people? The band, stretching out "Let's Take It to the Stage," has been on for a good forty-five minutes when I'm finally beckoned. I'm led outside and onto an herbalicious bus sporting a big-screen TV from which a good chunk of *The Hunt for Red October* unfolds, and, eventually, George Clinton, smile pasted, ambles from the back and sits a foot in front of me, clearly in no rush to take his ass to the stage.

Alright, this is probably a stupid question, but being that you are funk incarnate, how you would define funk?

Oh my God! You mean, how would I define funk today? Oh God. Funk is anything it needs to be today. Funk is like the Force. You do the best you can and after that, funk it. You have to do the best you can first, then let it go. Whatever happens, happens, but you have to trust it. It can be any kind of music. There's all kind of funk. Every folk got its own funk; every ghetto got its own funk. It's like when you're free and you don't mind what you look like, what you sound like, you let go. Today, our funk—because of all this bullshit goin' on in the world—may sound a little angry, but as long as you can dance to it, it's cool, funk it. You do the best you can and just let it go. So if it gets a little wild tonight [and we] take our dick out and shake it, don't worry about it. [*laughs*]

The biggest acts that usually roll through here are bands like Air Supply.

[*laughs*] Hey, we all gotta breathe! [*laughs*] They's pretty high too. We've been here before. We were here sometime in the '60s and shit. This ain't far from Newburgh; that's where we hid the Mothership when we rehearsed for the world Earth Tour and is also where we rehearsed for the Mothership Tour. It's got its own special bit of magic up here. I don't know what it is up here by Woodstock: some undercurrent vibe goin' on.

How do explain your longevity in the music game?

I like what I'm doin'. When you like what you're doin', it ain't a job. Matter fact, I have more fun than they do. When we play four hours, the first two and a half are for the folks who paid to get in. And little more than half of them might leave, 'cause they gotta go to work and all that shit. And the ones with the longer attention span last a bit longer. Then the ones left standing after that: they's for real! We play for them and each other. They really give you energy for the next night. Funk is like Viagra. [It's] Viagravation.

You don't need Viagra nowadays, do you?

[*laughs*] Ain't everyone needs it; it's just about havin' it! You wanna do the best you can. If that means knockin' the bottom out of it, then knock the bottom out of it!

How have your audiences changed over the decades?

In every conceivable way they could change. Blind, crippled, crazy, Black, White, tall, short, aliens… I mean, we've had every kind of audience imaginable. Depends on where we're going, depends on the time of year, we can't even tell. I don't even give the band a playlist. We gotta go out take a look, see who's there, say, "Okay, they'll probably dig this." We know what to do after about eight bars. Audience is *everything*. Which is what we wanted going from Parliament to Funkadelic. I said we'll never be trapped in another bag

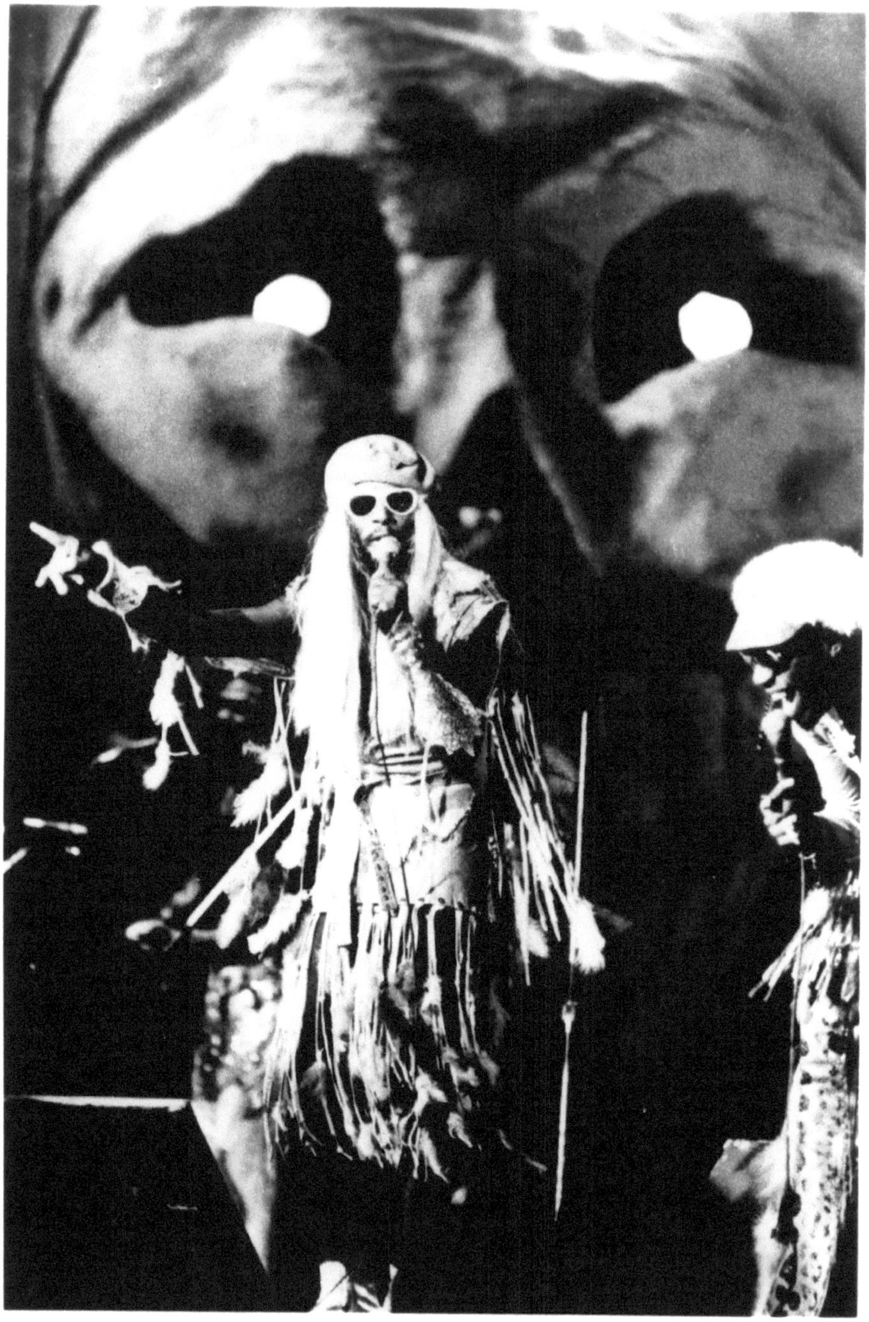

 **GEORGE CLINTON**
(REFEREE)

AUGUST 1979

again. Not even a nickel bag. We wanna be able to play and come out of whatever bag we feel like comin' out of. After "Testify" was a hit in '67, we made sure we made enough room for us so that by the time of *Free Your Mind…Your Ass Will Follow*, nobody would dare say, "Why'd you do that?" There ain't no reason, we just do it. And if that ain't enough, we got two, three groups we can do it with. That's why there's so many of us, so many variations. We like all kinds of music. My thing is: the more you can appreciate, the better off you are. Instead of someone gettin' on your nerve. If kids start liking something new, I don't say, "That ain't real music." I look for the music that the parents hate. I mean, you don't need no help to find fault. That's the easiest shit in the world to find. So if kids is likin' it—and kids *love* to like what you hate—then that means your appreciation is growin'. I mean, there was a time when feedback was noise. Jimi Hendrix took it to heaven. [*laughs*] I know what we did got on people's nerves! We'd test your attention span forever! But James Brown proved that if you stay in that groove long enough and get past that attention span part, it's like…[*squeals*] *whooo*, you're gone! Some people call it getting in the zone. Once you get past that part where you can't make it no further… And everything's got an attention span. Cars last three to five years. By that fifth year, if they ain't messed up, you'll try to mess it up. You'll try everything you can to try justifyin' buyin' a new car. A suit maybe has two years. A husband and wife have five, [*laughs*] know what I'm sayin'? You get past the fifth year, then in a few months you'll be wonderin', "Damn, why does it feel like I cannot go on further than this?" Sometimes, it overtakes you and you have to change up, but if you get past that point, it's like, "What the hell was I worried about? Anywhere I go I'll have some problems." So attention span is like that. You can best tell that on the highway when they fix the road, they fix this much of it. [*holds hands a foot apart*] It's called job security! Then they come back and fix the next part. They'll never just fix the road! [*laughs*] It's so easy to just do it. You go to Germany, I don't think they've messed with their highways since '45. They can do it as high tech as this world is. But they'd rather do it real slow. They'll tell a farmer not to grow corn this year to try to keep the price up. There's a reason for planned obsolescence: they want things to be obsolete. They build a new building every twenty-five to thirty years—I don't care how much money is spent on it. You look at the old city halls and Masonic buildings, they've been up there two hundred, three hundred years. They could do that if they wanted to. But they'd rather do it real slow and keep the price up and let other people starve and shit. There's a lot of work for everything that need to be done. Everybody could have a job. But they make you go through shit, all kinds of bullshit, so funk is funkin' with all of that!

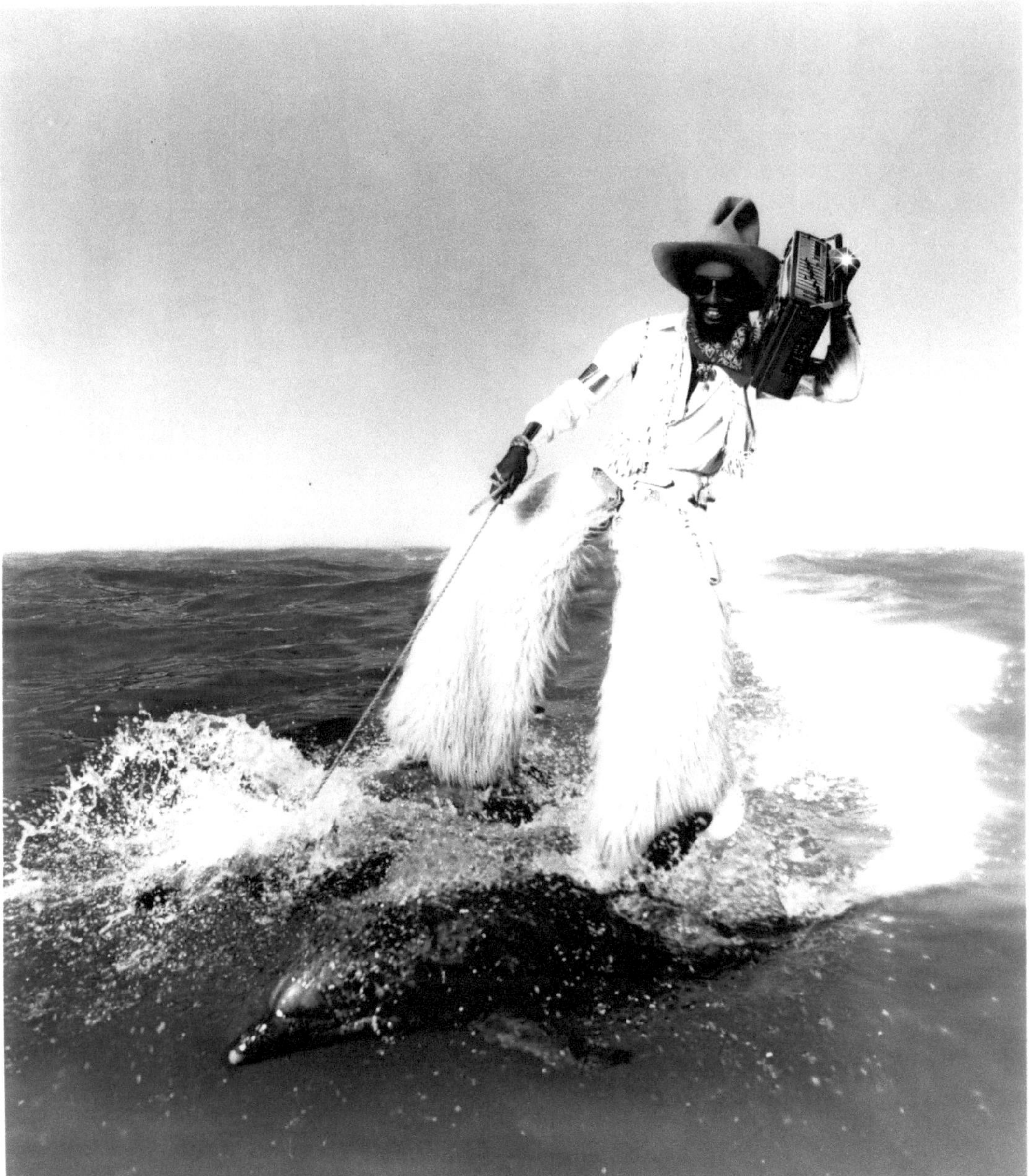

Casablanca Record and FilmWorks

PARLIAMENT

GEORGE CLINTON

DAVID LIBERT AGENCY

WORLD FUNK HEADQUARTERS

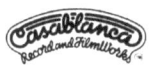

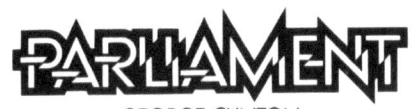

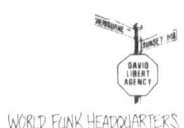

GEORGE CLINTON

(*top*) Setting up for the Mothership Tour at the Los Angeles Coliseum, 1977.

GEORGE CLINTON

Like in your song, "Whole Lot of BS."

Exactly. We still have fun doin' what we do. We can find a reason to go funk. If there are only ten people out there, we'll probably funk harder than we would if it was filled up. Just for the hell of it. And the last two out there, we'll beat their ass! We'll play songs we haven't played in twenty years just 'cause two of 'em are still there. Deadheads really give us a challenge though, 'cause they won't never go nowhere. It'll be daybreak! They'll be standing there—they'll be like this [*snaps his fingers arhythmically while imitating glazed Deadhead smile*] like we just started. "Okay, okay, okay! Shit!" Even when we play "My Girl" by the Temptations or, shit, disco, they give us a go for the money: they're the only ones.

Back in the '60s and '70s, you definitely transcended people pigeonholing you.

Before the Diaper Days was them suits. Couldn't never keep them clean and shit, couldn't keep our ties alike, our hair wouldn't stay done. So we saw muthafuckas with jeans on and with patches sayin' "Fuck you," and I said, "Damn! I can be poor-lookin'; that's easy! They getting away with that shit?" Man, we threw those suits in the back of the trunk, let the spare tire lay on them for a week or two, put them on again and we were cool as a muthafucka! And ever since then, it was like *sheee-iit.* We go to the Apollo Theater; people come in there and rob the dressing room; they take everyone's shit but ours! When that happens, you know you have no more problems. And we stayed that way totally funked out until, like, '77. Then we felt like, okay, part of us can go glitter again. But we didn't go back to the suits. No, we bought a three hundred thousand dollar spaceship and some ten thousand dollar leather suits and we became Clones. And you have to go back and forth to glitter, play both sides, and we had two groups so we could do both of them. But when we went glitter, we really went *glitter*! We went all the way. If you're gonna be commercial, then be *commercial*! And we're just about to do it again. We're gonna call it "Makin' Money"! We gonna show you how to make money. That's what the concept is gonna be about. We're gonna make it till it's obscene, then it'll be a brand new thing again. It'll be worth doin'. You don't have to steal, you just make the kind of music it takes to make money.

Nowadays, it seems either you're commercial or nothing.

But they're makin' some hard-core shit to be commercial, though. Eminem—he be beatin' the shit out of 'em and he's as hard as *hell*. I've been knowin' him since he was thirteen, fourteen. He beat the shit out of 'em and still makin' it commercial. They eatin' that shit up, and he ain't light, but it's good that way. Shit, the only way to make a bad word good is say it. You say it. If you say it enough, it won't be so bad. It's only when you stop sayin' it that it gets power. For example, you can't say a female dog is a bitch. What the kids gonna think? Kids are confused like hell. It's a bitch! That's what they should tell you. *Sesame Street* won't tell you that. "Stay away from drugs." But, hey, you can go to the drug store! What the fuck? What am I supposed to think? That's some oxymoronic shit. I don't know. Funk it. Just funk it. Do the best you can. It ain't meant to be bad. If it gets that way, it's 'cause someone wasn't payin' attention.

Seems like *America Eats Its Young* all over again.

All [civil] rights is in trouble right now, 'cause my man is goin' crazy out there right now. If everybody don't speak up soon we'll be like Germany [was]. He got into office and got away with it, now he's sayin' some shit that I know don't stand for what this country is supposed to stand for. You're supposed to be innocent till proven guilty. You don't go into someone's house and say, "I know he's in there and if you don't let him go, I'll bomb your house," then go to the next one and bomb that. You try that shit, you go to court and you go to jail. So it's a hell of a example that we're giving our kids. And what's scary is if another 9/11 happened right now, most people would agree with him. So we're in a real terrible spot, and I wouldn't put it past him to do it themselves [in order] to have the justification for doin' it. Everything about that stinks. How quickly we jumped on it as an excuse to run around the world…the evidence would've been thrown out of any court. People are just seeing [now] that it's fucked up. If something real tragic happened now, people'd get on his side and it'd be years before the world jump on our asses. If it's terrorists, I wanna know why the fuck they're that mad! The whole world's in trouble right now. *We've* got the weapons of mass destruction. Shit, if they've got it, we sold it to them. They should have a receipt! When you're pissed off, it's easy to go after anything. You gotta have some funk in you not to get mad.

What kind of music do you think George W. Bush listens to?

I don't know. I can't imagine. I would've liked to have known him when he was doin' blow. Probably was better off. He's put more people in the chair in Texas, and we believe someone like him will protect us? The Mafia at least tell you it's them…

As a songwriter, how've you changed?

I don't know. I don't know what to write about. You can't be out here preachin' that shit. I'm just runnin' my mouth now 'cause no one else will talk. You get in front of a lot of people and say shit now, they'll knock you off. Conspiracy is real. They're tryin' to do with [the word] "conspiracy" what they did with "liberal."

[*Just then, a fine sister in tight dress approaches from the back of the bus and begins working on George's hair. He takes a long look at the low end.*]

Damn!

On that note, thank you, Mr. Clinton. ●

After the succession of P-Funk interviews, New York writer and Wax Poetics *contributor* Matt Rogers *has aged ten atomic dog years, but is no more super stupid for the experience.*

Visit George Clinton at georgeclinton.com.

AUDIO HERITAGE
An Archival Perspective on Recorded Media
SUBJECT: Lacquer Discs (pt. 2 of 2)
by Brandon Burke // photos courtesy of the Library of Congress

Figure 1: A lacquer disc in process of delamination.

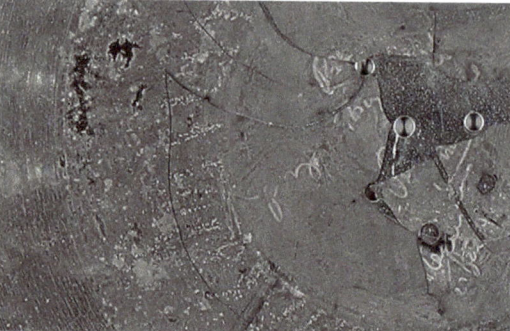

Figure 2: Palmitic acid appearing on a disc.

The simplest method by which lacquer discs degrade is everyday playback. Don't forget that the friction occurring between the stylus and the groove wall—the very same friction that produces the sound you hear in your speakers—is never anything short of destructive. This is especially the case with lacquers, since they are not solid like vinyl records but are, in fact, a nitrocellulose layer wrapped around and glued to a metal or glass core (or "substrate"). Consequently, every time you play a lacquer disc you erode that groove wall, edging closer and closer to the substrate with every spin. Once the substrate is exposed, it's only a matter of time before moisture and dust begin to compromise the adhesive that holds them together. This process is called delamination [*fig. 1*], and, once it begins, it cannot be reversed.

Two highly damaging processes occur due to the loss of castor in lacquer discs. Castor, it should be mentioned, is added to nitrocellulose as a softener, otherwise it would be too tough and brittle for manipulation by a recording lathe; but it never actually combines with the cellulose. Over time, as the castor begins to escape, the cellulose layer's mass decreases and it begins to shrink. The pressure the shrinking cellulose creates over the much stronger substrate—keeping in mind the fact that castor is the very stuff they added to make the cellulose softer in the first place—results in cracking and flaking on the surface of the disc. So running a needle over a delaminating lacquer disc, you can imagine, is like taking a knife over a wall with peeling paint. Bad news.

Castor loss can also result in palmitic acid [*fig. 2*], a white, oily, crystalline substance that is very difficult to remove. When palmitic acid is present on a disc that's *also* delaminating [*fig. 3*], you're basically screwed, because there's really no way to get that stuff off without applying both pressure and a liquid solution of some sort.

Cleaning lacquers at home is not recommended, especially since professionals use solutions containing independently purchased ingredients such as Triton xl-80n and alkyl dimethyl benzyl ammonium chloride. Not exactly Windex. So do like Pete Rock and think twice before you get yourself into a situation you can't reverse.

Store in a cool, dry environment somewhere in and around 50% humidity/70°F (21°C). (Remember, moisture accelerates the delamination process.) It is also recommended that these conditions remain as stable as possible. You know how string instruments go out of tune when you take them from a cold environment into a hot one, or vice versa? That expansion and contraction occurs among all organic substances, and, consequently, you don't want it here either.

Shelve vertically. Preferably in spaces tight enough to avoid leaning in any one direction, yet, at the same time, loose enough that you don't put undue pressure on them. Both can lead to warping. Avoid polyethylene-lined sleeves since plastics have a tendency to bond if in contact with one another for extended periods of time. Instead, try using an acid-free paper liner with a fold-over lip to seal out dust. They can be purchased anywhere professional archival supplies are sold. ⬤

Figure 3: A delaminating disc with palmitic acid.

www.ingramcontent.com/pod-product-compliance
Lightning Source LLC
Chambersburg PA
CBHW041547220426
43665CB00002B/55